LIFE

ARTIST'S

Michelangelo

Enrica Crispino

Michelangelo

Frontispiece:
Doni Tondo
(1503-1504/1506-1507),
detail, Florence, Uffizi Gallery.

Editorial Manager
Claudio Pescio

Graphics and pagination
Paola Zacchini

Editing
Sara Draghi
Augusta Tosone

Iconographic research
Cristina Reggioli

Transation
Silvia Silvestri

Editing of transation
Catherine Frost

www.giunti.it

© 2010 Giunti Editore S.p.A.
Via Bolognese, 165 - 50139 Florence - Italy
Piazza Virgilio 4 - 20123 Milan - Italy

First edition: June 2001
New revised edition: February 2010

Reprint	Year
9 8 7 6 5	2018 2017 2016 2015

MISTO
Carta da fonti gestite
in maniera responsabile
FSC® C023532
FSC
www.fsc.org

Printed by Giunti Industrie Grafiche S.p.A. –
Prato (Italy)

Contents

1475/1495 The making of a genius

FAMILY, YOUTH AND APPRENTICESHIP

Michelangelo's life is known basically through the two biographies written when the master was still alive, the one by Giorgio Vasari, from 1550 (reprinted in a second edition in 1568) and the one by Ascanio Condivi, dated 1553. The latter, a pupil of Michelangelo, claimed the absolute reliability of his biography, written under the master's direct control. More information on the artist's life is provided by letters to his relatives, with whom he always remained in close contact.

Michelangelo was born on 6 March 1475 in Caprese, near Arezzo. His father, Lodovico di Leonardo Buonarroti Simoni, was the Magistrate of this town and of the nearby Chiusi. But his mandate was about to expire and very soon the family moved back to their native town, Florence.

The young Michelangelo was then put out to nurse in Settignano, a village near Florence where the Buonarroti family owned property. The child's nurse was the daughter and wife of stonecutters, the activity for which the village was famous. From his nurse, Michelangelo was to say later, he had sucked in with the milk the art of sculpting, although this is hardly enough to explain the birth of a genius of sculpture.

Michelangelo began his artistic career against his father's will. In 1481, after the death of his wife Francesca Neri di Ser Miniato del Sera, Lodovico Buonarroti enrolled his son, then six years old, in the grammar school of Francesco da Urbino.

There Michelangelo learned to write, but caring little for Greek and Latin, suc-

ceeded at last in getting his father's consent to dedicate himself entirely to art. Michelangelo's first drawing may be the one of a male figure found in the Buonarroti house in Settignano. Although such mastery in a boy of thirteen or fourteen seems almost impossible to us today, precocity was quite common in the 15th century, as exemplified by Leonardo da Vinci or, in the field of literature, by a poet from the court of Lorenzo de' Medici such as Agnolo Poliziano.

In any case, there are no documents on Michelangelo's training in the sculptor's art, and strangely enough, it seems he was not engaged in a sculptor's workshop or with some corporation, as was the custom at that time. The only certain piece of information involving sculpture

is that between 1489 and 1492 the young master was admitted to the garden (no longer existing) of the Monastery of San Marco in Florence, where the precious collection of ancient statues owned by Lorenzo the Magnificent was kept. For this reason, it has been suggested that a possible master may have been the curator of the collection, Bertoldo, a pupil of Donatello who specialized in bronze sculpture.

Michelangelo's apprenticeship as a painter is instead more clearly documented.

Through a friend six years older, Francesco Granacci, who was already a pupil of Domenico del Ghirlandaio, Michelangelo entered the workshop shared by Domenico and his brother David. It was

Bertoldo di Giovanni,
**Bellerofon
and Pegasus**
(1481-1482),
Vienna,
Kunsthistorisches Museum.

Bertoldo di Giovanni,
**Hercules
on Horseback**
(1473?),
Modena, Estense Gallery.

Martin Schongauer,
**The Temptations
of Saint Anthony**
(c. 1470),
New York,
Metropolitan Museum.

Workshop of Ghirlandaio
(young Michelangelo?),
**The Temptations
of Saint Anthony**
(1487),
Fort Worth (Texas),
Kimbell Art Museum.

the year 1488, and Michelangelo was thirteen years old. His contract provided for a three years' stay in the workshop but, perhaps due to conflict with his master, he left within a year.

From the Ghirlandaio brothers Michelangelo learned mostly about drawing, copying the works of the Florentine masters from the recent past such as Giotto and Masaccio, but also those of foreign artists, as indicated by the report of a lost painting made from a print by Martin Schongauer.

And it was probably thanks to the Ghirlandaio brothers, engaged in those years in decorating the choir of Santa Maria Novella (Florence), that he first approached the fresco technique.

Then, in 1489, came a meeting of the utmost importance for him, an encounter with Lorenzo the Magnificent in the Garden of San Marco.

Palazzo Medici Riccardi in Florence.

Circle of
Andrea del Verrocchio,
**Bust of Lorenzo
the Magnificent**
(c. 1492),
Washington,
National Gallery of Art.

IN THE FLORENCE OF LORENZO THE MAGNIFICENT

In 1469 Lorenzo de' Medici, called the Magnificent for his political and diplomatic skills and for his generous patronage of the arts that was to make him the very emblem of 15th century Florence and of the Italian Renaissance, became lord of Florence.

Born in 1449 of Piero de' Medici and Lucrezia Tornabuoni, Lorenzo was the grandson of Cosimo the Elder, the founder of the Medici dynasty. After the early death of his father Lorenzo rose to power very young, at only twenty, inheriting an internal political situation still partially unstable, as demonstrated by the Pazzi conspiracy in 1478, but orientated towards the final consolidation of Medicean power. Following in the footsteps of his father and grandfather, Lorenzo did not officially appear as the political head of the Florentine State. The Medici family had always preferred to govern from "behind the scenes". Cosimo, as his son Piero and then Lorenzo were to do, played the role of private citizens, at most of "primi inter pares". Become a Signoria in all respects – although later than other Italian Comunes – Medicean Florence continued to proclaim itself a Republic. But it was only the appearance of the republican institutions that remained intact. In reality they were hollow inside, the most important magistracies being occupied by friends and faithful supporters of the family. Even the palace built by Michelozzo in Via Larga (now Via Cavour) for Cosimo, where Lorenzo continued to live, was an indirect confirmation of the family's deliberately low profile.

This residence, according to the original project (then modified over the centuries, especially in the 17th century), was not meant to be bigger nor more luxurious than the houses occupied by the major Florentine families of the time. In fact, similar or more magnificent buildings such as the Strozzi and the Pitti palaces were erected only a short time after Cosimo's palace, for clients as rich, or even richer, than the "Pater patriae". Nothing similar to the Palazzo Ducale of Urbino or the castle of Mantova was to be built by the Medici family in 15th century Florence.

With Lorenzo the Tuscan capital reached its highest splendour, imposing itself economically and culturally not only in Italy but all over Europe. On the one hand Lorenzo's city became one of the major financial and commercial centres (although the Medici's bank began to decline at the time of Lorenzo the Magnificent), on the other hand it became the cradle of the Italian Renaissance, the centre from which Renaissance culture irradiated.

In establishing this supremacy Lorenzo was crucially important for two reasons. In the first place, the period of prosperity and peace inaugurated in the Italian peninsula during the second half of the 15th century was the result of his diplomatic action. His great ability made him a mediator among the various Italian

Giorgio Vasari,
**Lorenzo
the Magnificent
among
the philosophers
and the men
of letters of his time**
(1555-1562), detail,
Florence,
Palazzo Vecchio.

States, always at war with one another, and a guardian of political balance in the peninsula. Considered for this reason "the needle in the scales" of Italian politics, he also forestalled, as long as he lived, the threat of foreign intervention in Italy. In the second place, his patronage of the arts encouraged an artistic flourishing of the highest level in the Florence of the time. A man of letters and poet himself, collector of precious objects and ancient statues in the famous Garden of San Marco, a fertile breeding ground of new talents, Lorenzo greatly promoted literature and the arts.

At his court lived and worked famous personalities such as Luigi Pulci, Poliziano, Marsilio Ficino, Cristoforo Landino, Pico della Mirandola. And in his service worked the greatest artists of the time, some of whom went to other Italian courts almost like cultural ambassadors of Lorenzo: Botticelli – a leader in the figurative culture of the period – Pollaiolo, Andrea del Verrocchio, Ghirlandaio, the young Leonardo and the very young Michelangelo, whom the Magnificent kept by his side, in the palace on Via Larga. As a patron, however, Lorenzo is not remembered for any unquestionable masterpiece, for any grand undertaking, the only exception being perhaps the magnificent Villa of Poggio a Caiano, by Giuliano da Sangallo. Incredibly, the greatest works from the height of the Laurentian season such as the *Primavera* and the *Birth of Venus* by Botticelli (c. 1482 and 1484) were not painted for him, but probably for his cousin Lorenzo di Pierfrancesco. Lorenzo de' Medici died at the age of forty-four, in 1492, the year America was discovered – two events that seem to mark symbolically the end of an epoch and the birth of a new era.

Giorgio Vasari,
Portrait of Lorenzo the Magnificent
(1533-1534),
Florence, Uffizi Gallery.

ART AND CLIENTS

The presence of a clearly-defined, well organized circle of intellectuals around Lorenzo, similar to those that formed in other Italian courts of the 15th century, brought with it a new element, with works of art now commissioned by the ruler and the city's most prominent families rather than by public institutions and religious orders. In effect, under the lord's rule the artist became essentially a court artist, working directly for the local ruler and living increasingly often in his palace. At the same time, his works were no longer produced mainly for the community, nor were they patronized by the major town guilds, as was still happening in the early 15th century – to mention one of the most famous cases – with the *Door of Paradise* sculpted by Ghiberti for the Florentine Baptistery, ordered by the Wool Guild. With the rule of the Medici family, commissions were more and more a prerogative of the ruler and his family, along with the other important families: Strozzi, Gondi, Sassetti, Tornabuoni, and Scala. Even when works of art were made for public buildings such as churches, they almost always ended up decorating the chapels of the nobility, conferring prestige on the families that had commissioned them: for example the frescoes by Ghirlandaio for the Sassetti Chapel in Santa Trinita or for the Tornabuoni Chapel in Santa Maria Novella.

Many more works were now destined to the private palaces and villas, built in ever increasing numbers starting from 1450, as can already be seen in the *Plan of the Chain* (1470), which shows a town much less bristling with towers than the one appearing in the surviving fresco in the Bigallo Loggia (1342), perhaps the most ancient view of Florence in our possession. For example, in Palazzo Medici can still be seen, in the Magi Chapel, the famous *Cavalcata* painted by Benozzo Gozzoli in 1459, while it is known that in Lorenzo's time his room on the ground floor was hung with splendid paintings, among them the three *Battles of San Romano* by Paolo Uccello, today divided among the Uffizi Gallery in Florence, the National Gallery in London and the Louvre in Paris.

Paolo Uccello,
**Battle
of San Romano**
(c. 1438),
Florence, Uffizi Gallery.

A cornelian gem
from Lorenzo's collection,
the so-called
Nero's seal
by Dioskurides
(1st century B.C.),
Naples, National
Archaeological Museum.

THE MEETING
WITH LORENZO DE' MEDICI
IN THE GARDEN OF SAN MARCO

When, around 1489, Michelangelo was taken to the Garden
of San Marco by his friend Francesco Granacci, his fellow
apprentice in Ghirlandaio's workshop, he was about fourteen years
old. There he found other young men who, thanks to their talent,
were also allowed to study the splendid Medicean collection.
Among these were the sculptors Pietro Torrigiano, Giovanfrancesco
Rustici, Baccio da Montelupo, Andrea Sansovino and the painters
Niccolò Soggi, Lorenzo di Credi and Giuliano Bugiardini
(and earlier, in the seventies, probably the young Leonardo da Vinci
as well). In the Garden of San Marco Michelangelo discovered his
real vocation for sculpture. And here Michelangelo was to keep
his appointment with destiny, a stroke of luck that would bring
the young genius under the direct protection of the Magnificent. The
anecdote describing the meeting between Lorenzo and Michelangelo
is one of the most famous among those reported by sources on
the sculptor's youth. Strolling through the garden, Lorenzo de' Medici
noticed the head of a Faun carved in marble. It had been sculpted
by the young Michelangelo who had copied an ancient statue,
ruined by time, representing a sneering old faun. The Magnificent
was impressed, but gently teased the young artist about the perfect
set of teeth he had put in that old man's mouth. Considering the age,
he should have lost some of his teeth, Lorenzo said playfully to
Michelangelo, called to his presence. Once alone, the already skillful
sculptor quickly modified his work by removing one of the teeth and
drilling the gums 'as if it had fallen out with the root', as reported
by Condivi. His fortune was made. Lorenzo returned, approved, was
pleased, spoke with Michelangelo's father and arranged to take
the boy to live with him in the palace in Via Larga, where he would
be seated at Lorenzo's table, among his children. For Michelangelo
this meant continuous contact with Lorenzo's erudite court:
with Poliziano, the tutor of Lorenzo's children, with Ficino

and Benivieni, and with Pico della Mirandola. And it also meant access to the magnificent collections of the Palazzo Medici, to the treasure of gemstones – carnelians, cameos and other finely engraved semi-precious stones – of medals and other rare and precious objects collected by the Magnificent which were to decisively influence him. No trace of the *Faun* sculpted by Michelangelo now exists. However it has been suggested that a mask once kept in the Bargello National Museum in Florence, now lost, was a copy of it.

Copy of the head of "Faun"
(once in the Bargello National Museum and attributed to Michelangelo, now lost),
Firenze, Casa Buonarroti.

Master close to Bertoldo and Michelangelo,
Bust of Satyr
(end of 15th century),
Florence, Bargello National Museum.

THE GARDEN OF SAN MARCO

The now lost Garden of San Marco, where Michelangelo first entered the world of sculpture, was located near the monastery of the same name. It was in the heart of the Medicean quarter, on Via Larga (now Via Cavour), where stood Palazzo Medici, and very close to the monastery whose prestige derived from the founder of the Medicean dynasty, Cosimo the Elder. The Garden of San Marco is linked to the name of Lorenzo the Magnificent. Within this space he created a magnificent collection of sculptures and ancient epigraphs (as well as 15th century works), allowing young artists to study them. The garden lay behind a building owned by the Medici family. The sources also mention a building with "loggia", "rooms" and "kitchen" inside the garden. Frequented already in 1475, this space was also used for a theatre, restoration workshop and scenery yard. The 15th century sources, Vasari in particular, speak of the Garden of San Marco as a proto-academy. According to indications from the oldest documents, this seems to be a strained interpretation. Probably Vasari stressed the function of Lorenzo's garden to accredit it as a forerunner of the Accademia del Disegno established in 1563 at the desire of Duke Cosimo I. In reality the Garden of San Marco seems to have resembled neither an academic institution nor a workshop. It served instead as a training ground for talent, in the generic sense of a stimulating context in which young men could meet artists and men of letters, talk and work inspired by splendid examples of ancient art and a curator of the collection – Bertoldo – who had been apprenticed to Donatello. The garden was also an important centre for the irradiation and promotion of Lorenzo's cultural policy. This "breeding ground for talents" must have been very important to the Magnificent who, it seems, was accustomed to finance the young men who frequented the garden with salaries and bonuses.

Present-day view of a corner of the Florentine Piazza San Marco: the cypress trees on the right stand in the area where the Medicean garden once was.

THE ARTIST'S WORKSHOP IN FLORENCE

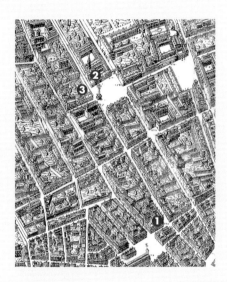

Stefano Buonsignori,
Plan of Florence
(1584), detail:
1. Palazzo Medici
2. San Marco
3. Medicean garden.

In Renaissance Florence, the workshop was the place where artists were trained. But it was also a profitable business that, established by an affirmed master assisted by pupils under his direction, produced complex works such as large cycles of frescoes and numerous works of art, all with the warrant of quality expected of such masters by the clientele. Apprentices usually entered the workshop very early, at about the age of ten. During the first year of apprenticeship they acquired basic technical knowledge. At first an apprentice was assigned almost exclusively to drawing: silver point or ink on white paper drawings or tempera on coloured paper. The teaching did not focus on theoretical knowledge but on those practical accomplishments that, in the shortest possible time, would allow the apprentice to work actively beside his master. The typical workshop did not provide qualification in any specific branch of art, but made its apprentices experts in a wide range of techniques – drawing, painting, etching, sculpturing, and goldsmithry. In 1488, when Michelangelo entered one of the most famous workshops of the time, that of Ghirlandaio, Florence numbered many others, such as that of Cosimo Rosselli, to mention one of the most important, where artists such as Piero di Cosimo, Fra Bartolomeo and Mariotto Albertinelli served their apprenticeship. Exemplary of the late 15th century workshop was the famous one headed by Verrocchio (1435-1488) whose apprentices included Leonardo da Vinci, Perugino, Botticelli and Lorenzo di Credi. Equally important among the workshops of the second half of the 15th century was that of the brothers Antonio and Piero del Pollaiolo.

THE CULT OF ANTIQUITY IN THE RENAISSANCE

The Swiss scholar Jacob Burckardt, in his famous essay written in 1860, coined the term "Renaissance" to indicate a new way of feeling and making art that developed in Italy in the 15th and 16th centuries.

Florence was the city from which the new trends, centering around two fundamental ideas – the revival of the classical world and the orderly application of the perspective method – irradiated. In reality the Italian artistic and cultural panorama in the 15th and 16th centuries appears upon close examination to be much more varied and complex, still marked by close ties to the Medieval world. However, a passion for antiquity and the discovery of perspective appear to be the salient features of Renaissance culture.

As concerns the "revival" of Greek and Roman art, it can be stated that the Renaissance basically focused on and brought to maturity the heritage of Humanism, that current of thought which already in the 14th century, with Petrarch, viewed the rediscovery, study and imitation of the classical texts (the "humanae litterae") as a fundamental element of the highest cultural milieus.

Contrary to what might be thought, the revolutionary aspect of this rediscovery did not consist of a return to reading the classics. Classical literature was certainly not unknown to the Middle Ages, as shown by Dante's veneration for Virgil. But with Humanism the lesson taught by the classics and their interpretation changed, revolutionizing the cultural viewpoint of the times. While in the Middle Ages, in fact, the ancient works were read in an allegorical key and placed within the contemporary Christian vision of the world, in Humanism and in the Renaissance the examples from the past nourished instead a reborn trust in man's

capacity and in his action in history, becoming not merely a model for art but also for life itself.

This is especially true for the Humanists of the first generation, from Coluccio Salutati to Matteo Palmieri to Giannoz-

Ascension of Saint John the Evangelist (c. 1490), copy from Giotto in Santa Croce, Paris, Louvre, Département des Arts Graphiques.

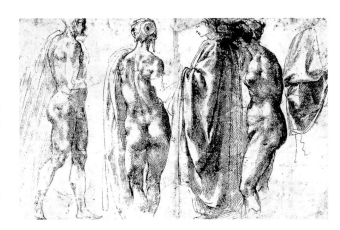

Five studies of statuary (1480-1501), Chantilly, Musée Condé.

zo Manetti, Leon Battista Alberti, Leonardo Bruni, Poggio Bracciolini and Lorenzo Valla, with their strong civil and political commitment.

In the second half of the 15th century instead, deference to ancient art as "magi-

stra vitae" declined and the classical ideal was pursued above all as the formal model of perfection and absolute harmony, the basis of an art and a culture destined to become increasingly elitist, remote from everyday life, arriving at the point of a sharp split between intellectual values and reality.

In spite of its very strong evocation of the past, Renaissance art never fell into the trap of cold imitation, nor sterile nostalgia. The classical models were not imitated in stale copies, but were taken as inspiration to act in the present and to express topical contents through new means. Imitation of antiquity did not mean counterfeiting or, worse, plagiarism; it was rather emulation, an effort to equal or to surpass an illustrious precedent.

When sculptors such as Donatello and Michelangelo drew inspiration for their works from classical sculpture, their aim was not that of making fake antiques, but of sculpting works of modern, original conception.

The spirit of Renaissance art was authentically new, marking a decisive change from the art of previous centuries. The great technical and thematic achievements of the Italian Renaissance were immensely successful, spreading rapidly throughout Europe to become an invaluable example for the artists of the next generations.

THE MYTH OF CLASSICISM IN FLORENCE AND ROME

Trained in Lorenzo's Florence, Michelangelo worked in this city and in Papal Rome, two capitals of the Renaissance where the new cultural myths, the new passions and trends, such as the cult of Classicism, flourished. In Florence and Rome lived and worked, in the early 15th century, the most eminent Humanists of the first generation – Bruni, Salutati, Bracciolini, Filelfo and Valla. Florence reigned supreme, for the entire 15th century, as the foremost center of art and culture. The fascination exerted by classical civilization is demonstrated by numerous rediscoveries of ancient codes, tenaciously sought by the Humanist men of letters who collected and studied them with passionate interest. Moreover, in artistic production, themes and stylistic features linked to the classical world flourished, from the architecture of Alberti and Brunelleschi to the sculpture of Donatello, from the mythological paintings of Piero di Cosimo, Pollaiolo and Botticelli to the poetry of Poliziano. These last two artists were among the leading figures at the court of Lorenzo the Magnificent, where the myth of classicism became tinged with new elements, influenced by the philosophic theories of Marsilio Ficino, scholar and divulger of Plato's works. Basic to

Farnese Hercules, Roman copy from a Greek original, Naples, National Archaeological Museum.

Farnese Bull,
Naples, National
Archaeological Museum.

his thought was the intention of integrating Christianity and Platonism. This explains the massive introduction of Neo-platonic motifs in the artistic production of the Laurentian circle and the birth of most unusual hybrids, works in which Neo-platonic meanings are superimposed on themes and subjects from the classical repertoire.

Exemplary of this trend are Botticelli's early paintings, primarily the famous *Birth of Venus* and *Primavera*. To complete the picture of Florence as lover of classical art, it should be recalled again that Lorenzo de' Medici himself was an ardent collector of ancient objects and sculptures, the latter kept in that now-lost Garden of San Marco to which the very young Michelangelo was admitted. In the 16th century, supremacy as capital of contemporary culture passed from Florence to Rome.

Here traces of the past were a concrete reality within the urban fabric and already for some time travelers had been visiting Rome to study the ancient ruins and the monuments of classicism (a famous example is that of Bernardo Rucellai, a member of the Medici entourage, who reported on his journey to Rome in 1471 with Lorenzo de' Medici and other friends, guided by Leon Battista Alberti).

In 16th century Rome the collecting of statues and antiquities became habitu-

Copy of a figure
from the "Tribute"
by Masaccio
(1488-1495),
Munich,
Kupferstichkabinett.

Masaccio,
Tribute
(1427), detail,
Florence, Santa Maria
del Carmine,
Brancacci Chapel.

marble bas-relief by Michelangelo's hand, in height just less than an arm, in which, being a young boy at that time, and wishing to imitate Donatello's manner, he acted so well, that it seems made by the hand of the latter'. Now Michelangelo's debt to Donatello is certain. And how could it be otherwise, considering the supremacy of the artist who still in Michelangelo's day was deemed the greatest sculptor of the 15th century, to be taken as a model like the classics? Yet as regards the Madonna of the

Stairs, Vasari's opinion seems too radical. The technical affinity, it is true, exists; but it is limited to the "stiacciato". What is lacking in Michelangelo's bas-relief is in fact the rigorous perspective scheme typical of Donatello's works. This is an important difference, since it demonstrates, along with other elements, the profound difference in the ideals and expressive values of the two artists. Donatello was in fact an artist of the early Florentine Renaissance, season of a renewed faith in the capacity of man, measure of all

Attributed to Michelangelo,
Garland-holder Putto,
in the crowning
of the Annunciation altar
in Sant'Anna dei Lombardi,
Naples, by the workshop
of Benedetto da Maiano
(1489-1492).

the things. His works were produced at a time of enthusiasm and certainty, a time when the laws of perspective were discovered and developed, organizing reality according to the meter of human rationality and becoming the basic principal of Renaissance art as a whole. Michelangelo instead grew up in the Florence of the mature Renaissance, where the philosophy of Marsilio Ficino brought back into the foreground a spiritual-religious approach to reality. Obviously Michelangelo could not avoid the perspective scheme, become by then ineluctable, but its rigorous application is not among the fundamental tenets of his art, and on the contrary it seems that Michelangelo was really irritated by long perspective studies. For him the representation of reality was primarily symbolical, spiritual and mystical. In his works a style was forming that would be the prelude and the direct antecedent of Mannerism, with its unnatural colours and the equally unrealistic twisted, elongated bodies.

**Madonna
of the Stairs**
(c. 1490),
whole and detail,
Florence,
Casa Buonarroti.

Donatello,
**Del Pugliese-Dudley
Madonna**
(c. 1440),
London, Victoria
and Albert Museum.

Donatello,
**Banquet
of Herod**
(c. 1435),
Lille, Musée
des Beaux-Arts.

In comparing the bas-relief of the *Madonna of the Stairs* with Donatello's *Madonnas*, Michelangelo's conception can be seen to differ also in composition and iconography. In Michelangelo's relief Mary does not turn her loving gaze toward the son she is nursing, but seems absorbed in thought. Moreover, the Child is portrayed from the back, an unusual iconographic effect. His muscles are out of proportion, his body resembling that of a little Hercules; lastly, his twisting motion fills the space in a way that is already far from the typical 15th century style. Then there is the added element of the stairs, with an obvious symbolic meaning. The scene as a whole, as well as its details, has been variously interpreted and references to different models and sources have been found. The Child, for example, has been compared to the classical statue of the *Farnese Hercules*, while the symbolic stairs recall Ficino's theory of the five levels of being (five like the steps carved by Michelangelo) and his stairs of love linking the worldly and the divine. A parallel may be found in a work composed in 1495 by Domenico Benivieni, Ficino's friend, who in the *Stairs of Spiritual Life above the Name of Mary* compares the five letters of the name Mary to the five steps of the stairway.

The *Battle of the Centaurs* relief, carved by Michelangelo between 1490 and 1492, has also been interpreted from a Neo-platonic point of view.

According to this hypothesis, it represents a "psicomachia", a battle between the animal and the spiritual components of the soul. In his biography Condivi states that it was Poliziano, an outstanding personality in the Laurentian circle, to suggest to the young sculptor this classical subject, which reflected the love of antiquity typical of the Medicean cultural milieu. Probably Michelangelo was generically inspired by precedents such as the *Battle* by his presumed master Bertoldo, or by an ancient Roman sarcophagus in the graveyard of Pisa. But his work already shows a very personal imprint and a mature style more reminiscent of a model chosen by the young genius against the general trend and in full autonomy – the pulpit by Giovanni Pisano in the Baptistery of Pisa.

The theme of the relief, recalled by Condivi as the *Rape of Deianira and the Fight of the Centaurs*, seems to offer the sculptor primarily an opportunity for a thorough study of the nude. The tangle of bodies portrayed in all positions was to provide the artist with an unlimited repertoire to be employed throughout his career.

Because of the background left undefined and the lack of a frame, the *Battle of the Centaurs* may be considered

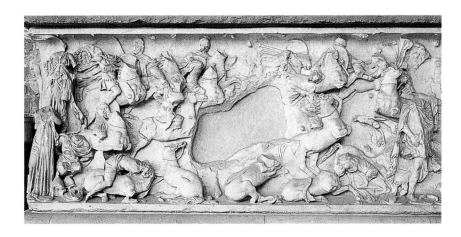

Roman sculptor,
**Sarcophagus
with battle scenes**
(2nd century A.D.),
Pisa, Camposanto.

Michelangelo's first "unfinished" work. Condivi, who mentions it as a work completed by the time of Lorenzo's death in April 1492, does not explain whether it should be considered purposely "unfinished" by the artist or whether this was due to an interruption caused by Lorenzo's death, when Michelangelo, shocked, left Palazzo Medici to return to his father's home.

Lastly, a polychrome wooden *Crucifix* is also included among the artist's youthful works, although its attribution to Michelangelo is controversial.

This work is a *unicum* in the artist's production, no other wooden sculptures by him being known. It is dated somewhere between April 1492 and October 1494, the span of time elapsed between Lorenzo's death and Michelangelo's escape from Florence a few weeks before the expulsion of the Medici.

The figure of Christ is evidently influenced by anatomical knowledge that is not purely academic, and it is just between 1492 and 1494 that the artist conducted anatomical studies in the Monastery of Santo Spirito, where the prior gave him a room in which to dissect the corpses of those who had died in the monastery's hospital.

The style of the *Crucifix polychrome*, which may be interestingly compared to the wooden *Crucifix* by Donatello in Santa Croce, seems influenced by the preaching of Girolamo Savonarola, who stressed the vulnerable, defenseless aspect of Christ.

Antonio del Pollaiolo,
Battle of the Nudes
(c. 1460),
Chiari (Brescia), Morcelli-
Repossi Foundation.

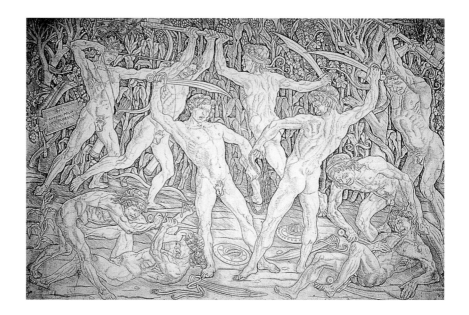

Attributed to
Pieter Paul Rubens,
**Battle
of the Centaurs**
(1600-1603),
from Michelangelo,
Rotterdam, Boymans-
Van Beuningen Museum.

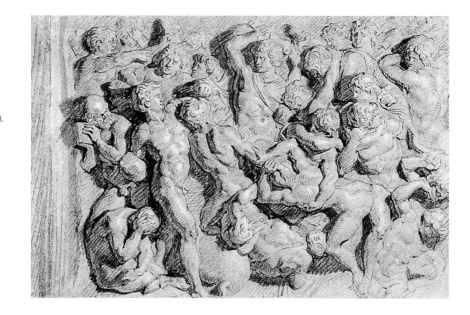

Battle of the Centaurs
(1490-1992),
Florence, Casa Buonarroti.

The relief is mentioned
by Ascanio Condivi (1553)
as a **Rape of Deianira
and the Fight
of the Centaurs**,
by Giorgio Vasari (1568)
as a **Battle between
Hercules and the Centaurs**.

1496/1506 The early masterpieces

Doni Tondo
(1503-1504/1506-1507),
detail, Florence,
Uffizi Gallery.

MICHELANGELO
IN LATE 15TH CENTURY ROME

Michelangelo's first stay in Rome dates from 1496, when the artist was a little over twenty-one. From the Republican Florence of Girolamo Savonarola, the young sculptor left for Papal Rome, reigned over by Alexander VI Borgia, who had been the target of the friar's harshest attacks, to which only one year later the Borgia Pope was to reply by excommunicating the Dominican.

What brought the future creator of the Sistine masterpieces to Rome that first time was the "fraud" of the fake *Sleeping Cupid* (now lost). This was a sculpture by Michelangelo, but so similar to an ancient statue that the merchant Baldassarre del Milanese managed to sell it to Cardinal Raffaele Riario, pretending it had been found in an excavation.

Later, having discovered the incredible falsification, the Cardinal had demanded reimbursement of the amount paid. However, he had also expressed a desire to meet the author of such an exploit, welcoming him into his own circle.

From a stay in Rome, Michelangelo had much to gain.

Meanwhile he kept his distance from the increasingly critical situation of Florence, where without a doubt – although Michelangelo himself was an admirer of Girolamo Savonarola – the friar's religious fanaticism was making the political and social situation increasingly tense and was preventing the free development of art and patronage, subjecting all artistic production to severe censoring.

In Rome, moreover, Michelangelo could refine his technique by studying at first hand the remains of classicism and ancient statuary, favored also by the recent trend sweeping through the wealthy, erudite circles of the late 15th century, that of forming their own collections of antiquities.

And lastly, Michelangelo could find excellent chances for work and success in a city that, thanks to him and to the new Pope Julius II, was to become the focal point of Renaissance art in the 16th century.

But now, at the end of the 15th century, Rome offered him no real competition, considering that Alexander VI employed good artists, but certainly not on the same level as Michelangelo, such as Pinturicchio (who had frescoed the Papal apartments in the Vatican Palace), and the sculptor Andrea Bregno.

Moreover, Michelangelo was undoubtedly helped by being received into the circle of Cardinal Riario, which also included several Florentine bankers who had settled in the Papal city.

Among these Jacopo Galli in particular was a very active patron of Michelangelo. The banker, highly influential in Rome, owned a magnificent house in the city whose garden, a real outdoor "antiquarium", contained a fine collection of ancient and modern works of art, as shown by a 16th century drawing by the Flemish artist Maarten Van Heemskerck. In this garden filled with antiquities Jacopo Galli had placed a sculpture by

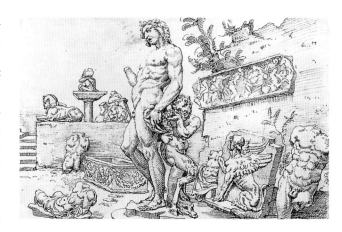

Michelangelo, the Bacchus, as can be seen in the drawing.

The statue (now in the Bargello Museum in Florence) had been sculpted for Riario and then sold to Galli when the Cardinal no longer wanted it. Galli also purchased another work by Michelangelo, known from the ancient sources as an *Apollo* or *Cupid*, which recent studies have identified as the *Young Bowman* now located in a building occupied by the Cultural Bureau of the French Embassy in New York.

Lastly, it was Galli who obtained for the sculptor the commission for the *Pietà* of Saint Peter's in the Vatican, the first truly famous work by Michelangelo, the masterpiece that consecrated him as a great artist in the eyes of his contemporaries.

Maarten van Heemskerck, **The garden of the Galli villa in Rome** (1532-1535), Berlin, Kupferstichkabinett.

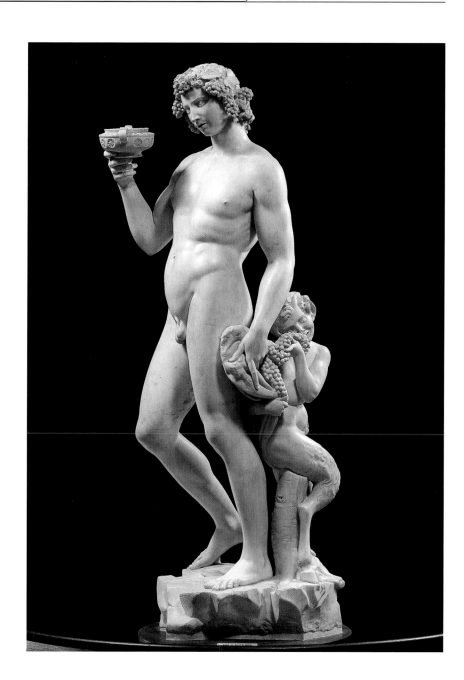

Bacchus
(1496-1497),
Florence, Bargello
National Museum.

"THE SLEEPING CUPID"

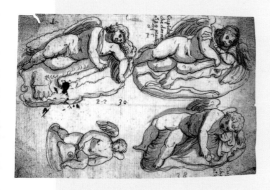

Drawings of statues, copies of the **Sleeping Cupid** by Michelangelo, from *Busts and Statues in Whitehall Garden* (17ᵗʰ century), Windsor, Royal Library.

Manchester Madonna (c. 1495-1497), detail, London, National Gallery.

All trace of this statue by Michelangelo was lost after it entered the collection of Isabella d'Este in Mantova. Since the Gonzaga collections were sold mostly to the English crown in the 17ᵗʰ century, it is probable that Michelangelo's statue was destroyed, along with other treasures, in the burning of Whitehall Palace in 1698. A *Sleeping Cupid* now in the Corsham Court collection, Wiltshire, is believed to resemble the original. When Michelangelo's *Cupid* was sold to its first buyer, Cardinal Riario, the marble was probably aged to make the work even more credible as an ancient piece of art; the idea probably came from an important Florentine patron and client of the sculptor, Lorenzo of Pierfrancesco de' Medici. He and his brother Giovanni were second cousins of Lorenzo the Magnificent. The two brothers, exiled by Lorenzo de' Medici's son, Piero, and then welcomed back to Republican Florence after the incapable heir of such a famous father had been banished by popular acclaim in 1494, had both assumed the epithet of Popolano. For Lorenzo of Pierfrancesco (died in 1503) Michelangelo had also sculpted an *Infant Saint John the Baptist*, now lost. But the most famous among the commissions of Lorenzo's cousin is still the *Primavera (Spring)* painted by Sandro Botticelli, which at the mid-15ᵗʰ century was in Lorenzo of Pierfrancesco's villa at Castello, near Florence, along with the no less famous *Birth of Venus* by the same artist.

Sandro Botticelli,
**Madonna
of the Pomegranate**
(1487),
Florence, Uffizi Gallery.

Young Bowman
(before 1494),
New York, Services
Culturels de l'Ambassade
de France.

Luca della Robbia,
Choir
(1431-1438), detail,
Florence, Opera
del Duomo Museum.

Manchester Madonna
(c. 1495-1497),
London,
National Gallery.
The standing angels
reveal the influence
of similar figures
by Botticelli
and Luca della Robbia.

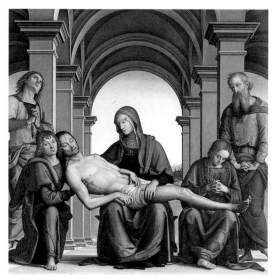

THE VATICAN "PIETÀ"

The *Pietà* in Saint Peter's is the first Roman commission of great importance assigned to Michelangelo and it is also the only work with his signature, engraved on the band that crosses the Madonna's bust bearing the words 'MICHAELANGELUS BONAROTUS FLORENT[INUS] FACIEBAT'. The famous marble group was commissioned by the French Cardinal Jean Bilhères de Lagraulas, ambassador from the King of France to Pope Alexander VI, who stipulated the contract with the intermediation of Jacopo Galli in 1498.

The *Pietà* was originally destined to the Cardinal's tomb in Santa Petronilla, an early Christian chapel annexed to the Constantinian Basilica destroyed to build Saint Peter's, where the *Pietà* was later to be placed. Vasari writes about the Christ: 'Do not think it possible to find a death scene more realistic than this. Here there is a very tender posture of the head, and such a concordance in the muscles of the arms and those of the body and the legs, the finely worked wrists and veins, that we are amazed that a man has been able to make so divinely and well such an admirable thing in an extremely short

Perugino,
Pietà
(c. 1493-1494),
Florence, Uffizi Gallery.

Raphael,
Transport of Christ to the Sepulchre (Baglioni Altarpiece)
(1507-1508),
Rome, Borghese Gallery.

Pietà
(1498-1499),
Vatican City,
Saint Peter's.

time'. And here is how the other famous biographer of the artist, Ascanio Condivi, describes the Virgin: 'Sitting on a stone, where the cross was raised, with her dead son on her lap, of so great and rare beauty, that anyone seeing it is moved to piety'. From these few words alone the salient features of this superb work appear evident: on the one hand the sculptor's ability, the technical virtuosity that lingers on the meticulous, flawless rendering of anatomical details; on the other, the dignified beauty of the figures – especially the gentle young Virgin – the touching poetry of a sculpture so luminous as to seem made of alabaster rather than marble, so finely has the stone been worked. Never again in the production of this master of the "unfinished" was there to be a work so clean, so fully completed, that it might have been sculpted to demonstrate the achievement of a formal perfection from which the artist could then deviate. Another proof of his mastery is the fact that Michelangelo sculpted the *Pietà* from a single block of marble, without adding supplementary pieces. The sculptor selected the block himself in the Carrara quarries, supervising its transport to Rome, which took nine months. In this masterpiece, Mary gazes downward, absorbed in quiet grief, at her dead Son deposed from

the cross. With energy, her right hand supports him, although touching the divine body only through the shroud, while the left hand opens out in a gesture that seems to introduce the onlooker to the tragedy of the Redeemer's sacrifice. In the composition of this work a perfect balance is achieved between two originally contrasting volumes: on one side is the Virgin, seated and erect;

Deposition in the Tomb
(c. 1500-1501), London, National Gallery.

Kneeling Female Nude, study for the "Deposition in the Tomb"
(c. 1500-1501), Paris, Louvre, Département des Arts Graphiques.

he wished to suggest Mary's purity visually in her unfading youth.

The *Pietà* was completed in one year, being finished in 1499, the year of the client's death. In Michelangelo's sculpture the representation of the *Pietà* was to become a constant theme. This statue met with great fame, becoming a model for contemporary artists as well as those of the following generations. Raphael was one of the first to draw inspiration from the *Pietà* for his *Baglioni Altarpiece*, while later painters such as Caravaggio and David, in the *Deposition* and in the *Death of Marat*, were to recall this work, especially as regards the arm of Christ.

Caravaggio,
Deposition
(1602-1604),
Vatican City,
Pinacoteca Vaticana.

on the other is Christ, whose naked body, lying in his mother's lap, is balanced by the ample drapery of the Madonna's skirt, so that the two figures seem inscribed in a single compact block. Today, as in the past, the Virgin's extreme youth is puzzling. It is unusual in a representation of this kind, being unrealistic in comparison to the age of the dead Christ. Although we have no proof as to the reason, according to Condivi's biography Michelangelo maintained that chaste women remain young longer than others, as if

Jacques-Louis David,
Death of Marat
(1793),
Brussels,
Musées Royaux
des Beaux-Arts.

SAVONAROLA

Born in Ferrara in 1452, Girolamo Savonarola was the third son of Niccolò and Elena Bonacossi. In 1475 he became a friar in the Monastery of San Domenico in Bologna. His first stay in the Dominican Monastery of San Marco in Florence, to which his name is linked forever, dates from 1482. In 1490, after several years passed elsewhere, he was called back to the monastery by Lorenzo the Magnificent, becoming its prior the following year. From this time on his preaching, strongly prophetic and moralistic in tone, met with increasing popularity, as well as the esteem of many illustrious personalities, from men of letters such as Pico della Mirandola, Benivieni and Ugolino Verino to artists such as Botticelli, Andrea della Robbia, Filippino Lippi, and the young Michelangelo. When in 1494 Piero de' Medici, the son and heir of Lorenzo the Magnificent, was banished from Florence and the Republic was restored, Savonarola became the inspiring force behind a government strongly controlled by his followers' party, the so-called "Piagnoni" (the whiners). More radically than ever the city was conditioned by moral strictness, asceticism and the struggle against corruption, deviating into fanaticism. In 1497 the famous carnival with the "bonfire of the vanities" was held in Piazza Signoria, but this was also the year when the friar was excommunicated by Alexander VI. When, in early 1498, the Pope threatened an interdict on Florence, Savonarola's followers began to abandon him. On April 8 of the same year, a group of "Arrabbiati" (the angry), as one of the factions hostile to the Dominican was called, entered San Marco to capture Savonarola. This was the beginning of the end, followed by inquisition, trial and lastly burning at the stake, in the Florentine Piazza Signoria on May 23, 1498.

Fra Bartolomeo,
**Portrait
of Girolamo
Savonarola**

(c. 1499-1500),
Florence,
San Marco Museum.

REPUBLICAN FLORENCE

In 1492, following the death of Lorenzo, the Italian political situation again became unstable. The particularism of the Italian States and the short-sightedness of their rulers led to invasion by the French, which in 1494 marked the beginning of foreign expansion in Italy. For Florence, the offensive of Charles VIII had crucially important consequences, determining the downfall of the Medici. Piero de' Medici had in fact decided to respect the traditional alliance with the King of Naples against whom the French king was moving, claiming his dynastic right to the throne occupied by the Aragonese. Consequently, the Florentines viewed his advance with growing anxiety (it was at this time that Michelangelo, frightened, fled to Venice and then to Bologna). In this tense, dramatic atmosphere the apocalyptic preaching of Savonarola fell on fertile ground, bringing increasingly greater support to the Dominican friar and his ideas for a radical reformation. When Charles VIII arrived in the vicinity of Florence, Piero's ineptitude in treating with the foreign king caused a popular uprising that put Piero to flight and ushered in a Republican government. The soul of the Republic was of course Savonarola. During the four years of his supremacy the friar imposed a sort of theocratic dictatorship. Having aroused the opposition of Pope Alexander VI for his denouncement of the corruption of the Roman Curia, Girolamo Savonarola was excommunicated and in 1498, abandoned by the people, was burned at the stake as a heretic.

Gherardo di Giovanni,
Piero di Lorenzo de' Medici
(1489),
Naples, Biblioteca Nazionale.

After his death Florence continued to be a Republic, but evolved a form of government that provided for a Gonfalonier in whose hands all power was concentrated. In 1502 Pier Soderini was elected to this office. With him artistic commissions, strongly opposed in Savonarola's time, returned to favor, and it was under the Gonfalonier's rule that Michelangelo sculpted the *David*.

Francesco Granacci,
Entrance of Charles VIII into Florence
(second decade of the 16th century),
Florence, Uffizi Gallery.

Florentine unknown,
end of the 15th century,
The Execution of Savonarola in Piazza Signoria
(1498),
Florence,
San Marco Museum.

MICHELANGELO AND SCULPTURE

Saint Matthew
(1501-1504), detail,
Florence,
Accademia Gallery.

In a letter to the famous Florentine philologist and historian Benedetto Varchi, Michelangelo wrote: 'I mean by sculpture what is done by removing'. The other kind of sculpture, 'what is done by adding, is similar to painting', he added in the same letter.
For Michelangelo sculpting thus meant using his chisel on the marble to remove the superfluous, not to model a malleable material. Another important indication as to what sculpture meant to him is found in one of his poems, which states, 'The best of artists hath no thought to show / Which the rough stone in superfluous shell doth not include'. Michelangelo's attitude clearly shows the influence of Neo-platonic thought: the idea, the form of the statue was for him already contained in the marble, the chisel frees, manual work is at the service of spiritual revelation.
As a confirmation of the Neo-Platonic matrix of Michelangelo's concept of sculpture, here is this same concept as it appeared already in the 5th century in the writings of the Pseudo-Dionigese the Areopagite, the Christian philosopher who left a number of texts of Neo-platonic inspiration: 'The art of those who sculpt an image in stone which seems alive', wrote Dionigese, is accomplished 'by removing from it everything that prevents a clear vision of the latent form, revealing its hidden beauty only by removing the superfluous'.

Donatello,
David
(forth decade
of the 15th century),
Florence, Bargello
National Museum.

Andrea del Verrocchio,
David
(c. 1465),
Florence, Bargello
National Museum.

THE "DAVID"

In 1501 the twenty-six-year-old Michelangelo was asked by the Florentine Republic to sculpt a statue of great size representing David, the young shepherd who was to become King of Israel, the Biblical hero who had defeated the giant Goliath. During those years Florence was experiencing – after the artistic and cultural standstill under Savonarola, ending with the execution of the friar in 1498 – a new phase of vitality and of strongly promoted initiatives, especially since Pier Soderini had been elected Gonfalonier in 1502. The huge marble block from Carrara, used for the *David*, had in fact been excavated many years before and had already attracted the attention of the Florentine rulers, who had at various times considered having a statue sculpted from it.

Sketch for a "David with Slingshot"
(1501),
Paris, Louvre,
Département
des Arts Graphiques.

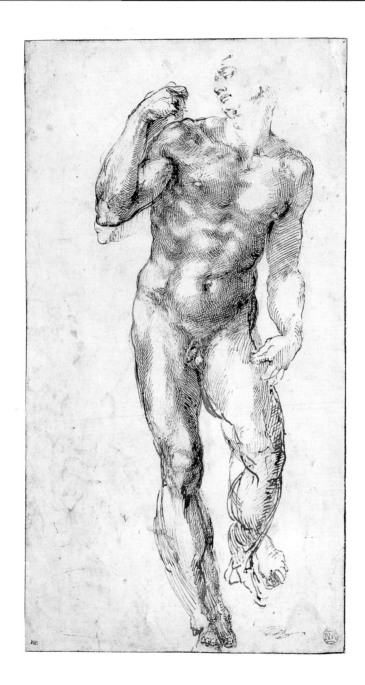

David
(1501-1504),
Florence,
Accademia Gallery.

In 1464 the task was assigned to Agostino di Duccio, but the contract was then cancelled for unknown reasons.

In 1475 the commission was given to Antonio Rossellino, who roughed out a statue but did not finish it. When Michelangelo accepted the task of sculpting the *David*, the block of marble was lying abandoned in the warehouse of the Opera del Duomo, the institution responsible for architectural and decorative works for the Florentine Cathedral, finished a little over half a century earlier with Brunelleschi's prodigious dome. The colossal statue was destined to one of the buttresses of Santa Maria del Fiore, calling for an imposing sculpture that could be seen well from below.

Michelangelo undertook to finish the work within two years against the payment of six gold florins per month.

But the work lasted longer than expected, both because the task was in itself difficult, and because the sculptor preferred to work alone, without assistants; another complication arose from the fact that he was working on a project already begun by someone else, rather than on virgin material. Finally, in 1504, the statue was ready. Such a monumental statue had never been seen since ancient times.

And Michelangelo sculpted it in a makeshift laboratory, set up in the vicinity of the Cathedral, where he remained to work day and night, quite happy to sleep a few hours on the floor, never leaving his work.

The *David* was so magnificent and huge that the original destination soon appeared unsuitable. To find the best location for that masterpiece, it was decided to ask the opinion of other famous artists of the times, such as Giuliano da Sangallo, Filippino Lippi and Leonardo da Vinci.

Finally it was decided to display the colossus, imbued with civic and political significance – since David fighting for the freedom of his people was a perfect symbol of Republican virtue – in Piazza Signoria, the centre of the city's political life.

But new questions arose as to where to put the statue: under the Loggia dell'Orcagna (later called dei Lanzi) or, as proposed by others, in front of Palazzo della Signoria, the solution that was then chosen. In front of the palace the original *David* remained until 1873 (its place was later taken by a copy) when, to save it from the ravages of the weather, it was moved to the Accademia Gallery, the Florentine museum where it still stands today.

In iconography, the *David* by Michelangelo clearly differs from the Florentine precedents of Donatello's *David* and the one by Verrocchio. The *David* by Donatello has in fact boots, helmet and

David
(1501-1504), detail, Florence, Accademia Gallery.

David
(1501-1504), detail,
Florence,
Accademia Gallery.

sword, while Verrocchio's also has a sword and boots as well as light clothing (according to the Biblical text).

Their bodies are slight and youthful; at their feet lies the severed head of Goliath. Michelangelo's *David* is instead nude like the statue of a Greek god, with only the slingshot thrown over his left shoulder. His body is that of a young man, and his task has not yet been accomplished (Goliath's head is missing). Michelangelo portrays David just before the conflict, displaying the tension of the moment in the taut face, the concentrated gaze, and the muscles ready to spring into action.

Michelangelo's choice seems a meditated one, all the more so as we know from the documents regarding the *David* that he had originally been asked to adorn the hero with a garland of golden leaves and a golden belt, according to a more traditional representation.

The sculptor has instead evidently modeled his *David* on a classical statue, although no precise model is known, thus renewing the dictates of contemporary sculpture where, as in other fields, the "modern" revealed itself through a purposeful and original revival of the past. Unlike the indubitably splendid *David* by Donatello, Michelangelo's masterpiece is magnificent viewed from all sides, not from the front alone. And considering the great size of the statue, its workmanship appears perfect.

As with all of the artist's other sculptures, a deep, thorough knowledge of the human body emerges, and the rendering of anatomical details is flawless.

The study of anatomy was another of the innovations that produced a change in the art of the period, a requisite shared by Michelangelo with another genius, always opposed by him, Leonardo da Vinci. The latter was to pursue his anatomical studies to the point of dissecting corpses (a bizarre practice at that time), even being accused for this reason of necromancy.

In this masterpiece, admired for five centuries, even the presence of a mistake (among the very rare errors found in Michelangelo's works) in one of the *David*'s wrists – where a muscle that does not exist has been added – proves to be functional from an artistic point of view, contributing to the plasticity of the effect.

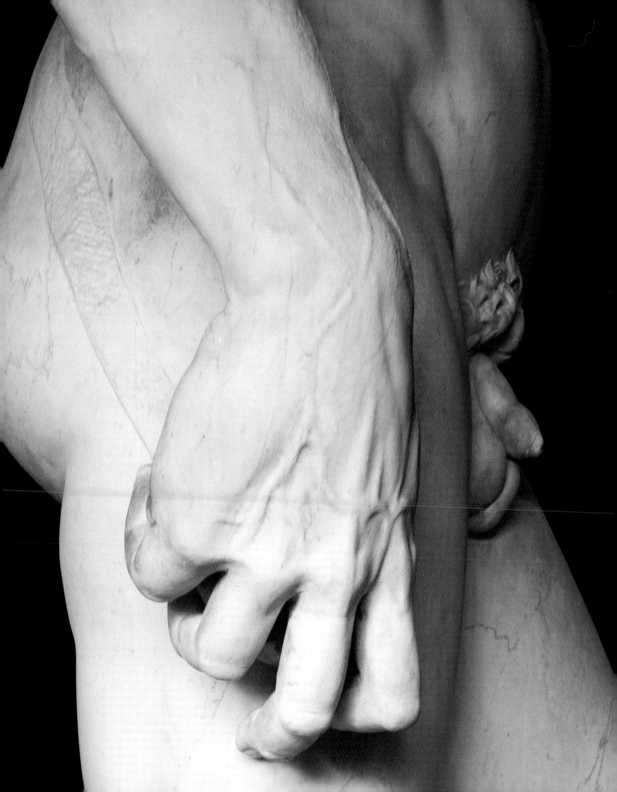

The **David** in the Tribuna of the Accademia Gallery in a photograph from the end of the 19th century: note the plaster casts of some of the artist's other works placed there at the time.

Below: Transporting the **David** from Piazza Signoria to the Accademia, from "Nuova Illustrazione Universale", no. 6, January 1874.

A MUSEUM FOR THE "DAVID"

In 1873, just after the Unification of Italy, the *David* was removed from Piazza Signoria and transported to the Accademia Gallery. Later it was replaced by a copy, while a bronze reproduction was placed in Piazzale Michelangelo. The new acquisition led to the creation, in the Florentine museum, of a Tribuna where Michelangelo's masterpiece would be worthily displayed. The project by the architect Emilio De Fabris – who completed the Tribuna between 1872 and 1882 – provided for a room in the shape of a Latin cross, with a round skylight below which the *David* was to be placed.

In 1875, two years after Michelangelo's statue had entered the Accademia, the Tribuna (although still unfinished) was chosen as the ideal place in which to display the great exhibition of reproductions of the artist's works which was to celebrate the forth centennial of the artist's birth. But in the early 20th century, the moulds of Michelangelo's work left in the museum, surrounding the original *David*, began to seem inappropriate. It was decided to collect a group of original works by Michelangelo in the Accademia.

In 1909 there arrived from other Florentine collections the *Captives*, until then displayed at the Boboli Gardens in Buontalenti's Grotto, where they had been placed by Grand Duke Cosimo I, and the *Saint Matthew*, which had stood in the courtyard of the Fine Arts Academy. Then in the late Thirties came the *Pietà from Palestrina*, from the city of the same name, which however is no longer attributed to Michelangelo by most of the experts.

David
(1501-1504),
Florence,
Accademia Gallery.

Saint Matthew
(1501-1504),
whole and detail,
Florence,
Accademia Gallery.

THE "DONI TONDO" AND THE "BATTLE OF CASCINA"

Due to the acclaim that met the *Pietà* in Rome, Michelangelo upon returning to Florence was bombarded with commissions, among them, as has been seen, the crucially important one for the *David*. The other works from this most intense Florentine period are: another bronze *David* (now lost) for the French Marshal Pierre de Rohan; the twelve *Apostles* commissioned by the Wool Guild for the Florentine Cathedral, of which only a *Saint Matthew* was to be roughed out; the *Madonna and Child* bought by the Mouscron family from Bruges for their chapel in the Notre-Dame church in the Flemish city; the *Pitti Tondo* and the *Taddei Tondo*, so called from the names of their clients, as well as the very famous work that introduced Michelangelo as a painter, the *Doni Tondo*; and lastly, the unfinished *Battle of Cascina*. The *Doni Tondo* is considered to be the only panel painting by Michelangelo, although some experts are also inclined to attribute to the artist a few paintings accomplished before the masterpiece now in the Uffizi, such as the so-called *Manchester Madonna*, now at the National Gallery in London (see p. 39) and – with more caution – the *Deposition in the Tomb* from the same museum (see p. 43).

Taddei Tondo
(c. 1503),
London, Royal
Academy of Arts.

The *Holy Family* of the *Doni Tondo* was painted for Agnolo Doni and his wife Maddalena Strozzi, perhaps on the occasion of their marriage, celebrated between 1503 and 1504 or, it has been suggested, some years later, between 1506 and 1507; in any case, some time around that 1506 when another great artist of the period, Raphael, painted splendid portraits of the married couple. The composition on a round support followed the most typical 15th century Florentine tradition, having been used, for example, in the *Madonna of the Pomegranate* by Sandro Botticelli (see p. 38) and the *Madonna of Humility* by Luca Si-

Pitti Tondo
(c. 1503),
Florence, Bargello
National Museum.

gnorelli, from which Michelangelo obviously drew some inspiration. In the *Doni Tondo*, however, Michelangelo's bold experimentation is already accentuated. In the first place, the iconography of the group with the Madonna twisting to receive, over her shoulder, the Child handed her by Saint Joseph, is unusual.

Raphael,
**Portrait of
Agnolo Doni**
(1505),
Florence, Pitti Palace,
Palatina Gallery.

Raphael,
**Portrait of
Maddalena
Strozzi Doni**
(1506),
Florence, Pitti Palace,
Palatina Gallery.

The Virgin's appearance too is atypical. Maria has strong, robust features and is portrayed without a veil, dressed in classical style with bare arms, a physiognomy that seems to anticipate the *Sibyls* painted on the ceiling of the Sistine Chapel. Then there are the colours: light and cold, harshly juxtaposed and iridescent, a color scheme that is a prelude to the palette revealed by restoration of the Sistine, in sharp contrast with the taste of the period for pleasing, harmonious tones. Moreover, the young nudes in the background recall the *"Ignudi"* painted on the famous ceiling of the Sistine.

Already in the *Doni Tondo*, as later in the masterpiece frescoed in Vatican, Michelangelo's work appears to be painted sculpture, with the holy group in the Uffizi panel showing a strong three-dimensional effect, its plasticity underlined still further by the sharp contrast between light and shadow. As regards its meaning, the Florentine painting seems to allude to the division of humanity before and after the birth of Christ. If so, the nudes in the background (note the low wall separating the Holy Family from the young men in the background) are not classical figures of shepherds, as in the painting by Luca Signorelli, but probably represent the pagan world before the Revelation.

To that world still belongs the Baptist, the infant Saint John who significantly leans against the wall and is the only one looking at the protagonists of the New Testament.

In 1504, having finished the *David*, Michelangelo was awarded another important public commission, the frescoing of the *Battle of Cascina* for the Grand Council hall – the so-called Salone dei Cinquecento – in Palazzo della Signoria. A few months before, the Republican government had commissioned another brilliant artist, Leonardo da Vinci, to paint the *Battle of Anghiari*, of which the *Battle of Cascina*, in the same hall, would have been the companion piece. In this way Florence intended to celebrate the present and past Republican glory by recalling two victorious clashes: the one fought between Florentines and Pisans at Cascina, in 1364, and that of Anghiari against the Milaneses, in 1440. To carry out this initiative the authorities called upon the two greatest artists in the city, challenging them to a duel in which each would do his utmost. The challenge appeared supremely interesting for many reasons, also because, as we know, there was bad blood between Michelangelo and Leonardo and now they would have to work together, at the same time, on two opposite walls. But in the end neither one nor the other finished his work. Not that they did not try; they both prepared extraordinary cartoons (now lost) for

Doni Tondo
(1503-1504/1506-1507),
Florence, Uffizi Gallery.

their frescoes, which were exhibited and judged superlative by contemporaries, then studied by several generations of artists from whose copies the originals may be imagined.

Curiously enough, the cartoon for the *Battle of Cascina* – called "the school of the world" by Benvenuto Cellini – was lost due to excessive use. Passed from one artist to another to be admired and copied, it was then dismembered into several parts and dispersed among various Italian courts, where the pieces literally wore out.

While Leonardo focused on the battle scene, on the violent impact of bodies and weapons, Michelangelo chose an episode related in the 14th century *Chronicle* by Giovanni Villani. He chose to depict the Florentine soldiers at the moment in which, camped near Cascina, they are bathing in the Arno river when suddenly the alarm sounds for the enemy's arrival, obliging the warriors to throw on their clothing and hastily search for their weapons.

Doni Tondo
(1503-1504/1506-1507), details, Florence, Uffizi Gallery.

This detail shows one of the small heads of the prophets adorning the frame, probably designed by Michelangelo himself, surely one of the few original ones surviving from the 16th century.

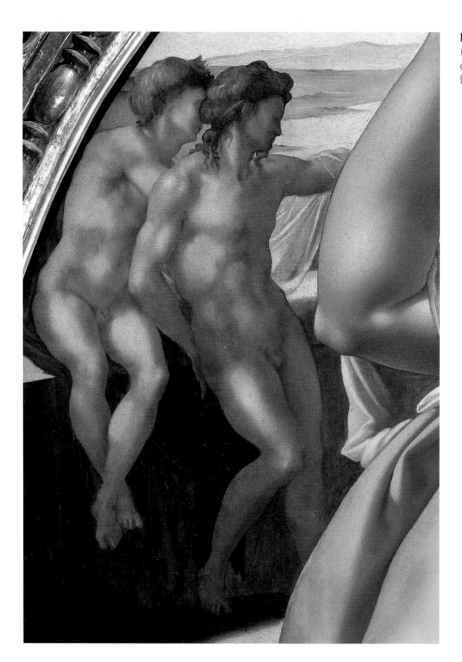

Doni Tondo
(1503-1504/1506-1507),
details, Florence,
Uffizi Gallery.

**Nude seen
from behind
and other sketches**,
probably for the
Battle of Cascina
(c. 1504-1505),
Florence,
Gabinetto dei Disegni
e delle Stampe,
Uffizi Gallery.

As in the youthful *Battle of the Centaurs*, the study of the nude seems once again Michelangelo's chief concern – the dynamism, energy and excitement of those vigorous bodies in their different responses to the surprise factor (Vasari admired above all the old soldier seated in the right foreground, who is pulling his trousers onto his wet legs as fast as he can). From the technical viewpoint as well, the differences are evident: Leonardo aimed essentially at a pictorial effect. Michelangelo instead, who always felt himself primarily a sculptor, drew a series of statuary figures of strong plastic impact.

In the end, the genius from Vinci was the only one to transfer part of his cartoon, the central core of the scene, onto the long wall of the Council Hall. Leonardo da Vinci had already painted the magnificent *Last Supper* in the refectory of Santa Maria delle Grazie in Milan, where the technique employed – only partially frescoed – was to prove unsatisfactory as regards duration. For the *Battle of Anghiari* the artist decided to ex-

Study for the "Battle of Cascina" (c. 1504-1505), Florence, Gabinetto dei Disegni e delle Stampe, Uffizi Gallery.

periment with oil colours. This was an immediate disaster, since the paint did not dry quickly enough but melted and dripped, spoiling everything. As for Michelangelo, he did not even put his hand to the brush. In 1506 the work of both artists was interrupted.

Leonardo left for Milan at the request of the French governor Charles d'Amboise, and Michelangelo went to Rome to fulfill the contract signed with Julius II, who had commissioned him to sculpt the statues for his tomb.

Bastiano da Sangallo,
Battle of Cascina
(c. 1542),
copy from the lost
cartoon of Michelangelo,
Norfolk,
Leicester Collection.

LEONARDO AND MICHELANGELO

The well-known rivalry between Leonardo and Michelangelo
was due both to the conflict between different generations
(Leonardo was twenty-three years older than Michelangelo)
and to a different mentality and irreconcilable artistic concepts:
on the one hand Leonardo's rationality, his rigorously scientific bent
and the priority he assigned to painting, on the other Michelangelo's
deep spirituality and his firm conviction of the superiority of sculpture.
A manuscript written near the middle of the 16th century, the *Anonimo
Magliabechiano*, reports the amusing episode of a clash between
the two greatest Italian artists of the day in the public street during
the time when they were both in Florence. The Magliabechiano
manuscript relates: 'The said Leonardo happening to walk
with Giovanni da Gavine from Santa Trinita [...] where a group
of gentlemen had gathered to discuss a passage from Dante, they
called Leonardo asking him to explain to them that passage. [...]
And Michele Agnolo happened to be passing by, and was greeted
by one of them; Leonardo answered: "Michele Agnolo himself will
explain it to you". Since it seemed to Michelangelo that this had
been said to ridicule him, he answered angrily: "Explain it yourself,
you who made a drawing of a horse to have a bronze cast
[the equestrian statue of Francesco Sforza never completed]
and you could not cast it and for shame you left it there". And having
said this he strode off, leaving Leonardo blushing at those words'.

Madonna and Child and Saint Anne (c. 1501-1502), Oxford, Ashmolean Museum, copy from Leonardo's cartoon for **The Virgin with Saint Anne and Child**.

Leonardo da Vinci, **The Virgin with Saint Anne and Child** (c. 1497), London, National Gallery.

$1507/1512$ **The Sistine Chapel: act one**

Delphic Sibyl
(1508-1512),
detail of the ceiling
of the Sistine Chapel,
Vatican City.

THE ROME OF JULIUS II

Early 16th century Rome, where Michelangelo was to firmly consolidate his fame, was dominated by the figure of Pope Julius II della Rovere. Raised to the papacy in 1503 as the successor of his bitter enemy Alexander VI Borgia, the new Pope worked with extreme determination to re-establish for the Papacy a leading position within the fragmented context of the Italian States and with the great European powers, and to restore the city of the Vicar of Christ to its past splendour. For this purpose, Julius II embarked on an expansionist policy marked by a series of victorious military campaigns and by a shifting game of alliances resulting in the Holy League against the French in 1511. In spite of his successes, the Pope's universalistic dream was soon to prove totally anachronistic.

Julius II's great mistake was to underestimate the political weight of the foreign powers involved in the conflicts between the Italian States. Later on it was to become clear that the fact of having transformed the Italian territory into a battlefield, freely allowing foreigners to interfere, had served only the purpose of helping the Spanish and French to gain control of the peninsula.

In parallel to his military exploits Julius II, dreaming of reviving the splendid magnificence of Imperial Rome, inaugurated a wide-ranging cultural policy, calling to his side the greatest contemporary artists such as Bramante, Raphael and Michelangelo. In this case the operation was fully successful and already in the first years of the 16th century Rome had become the supreme cultural capital of Italy, superseding Florence as the foremost city of Renaissance culture.

The Humanist Pope Julius II cultivated a love for antiquity in keeping with the taste of the age. His collection of classical statues in the Belvedere garden in Vatican City was one of the most precious collections among the many to be found in the noble palaces of families such as the Della Valle, Cesi, Sassi, and Farnese in 16th century Rome.

In one of these collections, that of Jacopo Galli – the banker who in 1498 had obtained for Michelangelo the crucially important commission for the Saint Peter's *Pietà* – was a work by Michelangelo, the

Raphael,
Pope Julius II in the "Consignment of the Decretals"
(1509-1511)
Vatican City,
Vatican Palaces,
Stanza della Segnatura.

Charles de Tolnay,
Reconstructions of Michelangelo's first (1505) and second (1513) designs for the "Tomb of Julius II".

Raphael,
Portrait of Julius II
(1512),
London, National Gallery.

statue of the *Bacchus* now at the Bargello Museum in Florence. This is proven by a drawing from around 1530 by Maarten van Heemskerck showing the statue in the garden of the Galli home, surrounded by antiquities (see p. 34).

As a client, then, Julius II promoted great works such as the rebuilding of Saint Peter's, an ambitious project commissioned of Donato Bramante.

The Pope then decided that his imposing tomb should be placed in the new cathedral. As designer of the project he thought of Michelangelo, whom he had met for the first time in 1505. This was that Tomb of Julius II with the famous *Moses* statue which, after enormous complications in its planning and realization, was to be placed in the church of San Pietro in Vincoli many years after the Pope's death. But among the papal commissions, two decorative works in particularly are crucially important. The first is the one commissioned of Raphael, called upon in 1508 to fresco the new apartments of Julius II in the Vatican Palaces. These are the paintings in the "Stanze Vaticane", with the famous masterpieces of the *School of Athens* and the *Liberation of Saint Peter from Prison*, where the first Bishop of Rome is portrayed with the features of the 16th century Pope. The second is the frescoing of the Sistine Chapel, where Michelangelo's genius was to be engaged from 1508 to 1512.

Tomb of Julius II
(finished in 1547),
whole and, right,
detail of the **Moses**
(1513),
Rome,
San Pietro in Vincoli.

THE FRESCO TECHNIQUE

The Sistine Chapel was decorated by Michelangelo "a fresco".
Frescoing is a technique of wall painting which consists of painting
on a plastered wall while the plaster is still damp (from which comes
the term "a fresco", meaning "while fresh"). With this technique the
colours chemically bind with the support, becoming, once dry,
indissolubly fixed to the surface on which they are applied.
Some preliminary operations are carried out to prepare the wall
to be frescoed. First it is treated with an initial layer of rather granular
plaster, called "rinzaffo"; on this is applied a second layer of still
quite rough plaster – the "arriccio" – on which the drawing can
be directly traced with charcoal and sinopia (a characteristic red
umber). Lastly, over the "arriccio" is applied a third thin, smooth layer
of plaster on which the artist paints, while it is still damp, with rapid
brushstrokes and with pigments resistant to the lime contained
in the basic plaster mixture. Since the latter dries very quickly,
the artist proceeds piece by piece, calculating the amount of surface
that can be painted in one day. It is thus possible to determine
how many days were needed to finish a certain work, by observing
the suture between two different portions of plaster.
It is clear that an artist who intends to practice fresco painting
must be able not only to foresee how much he can paint in one day,
but also to paint quickly and precisely (Michelangelo, for example,
worked very rapidly) in order to limit to a minimum any subsequent
modifications "a secco" (dry), which do not guarantee colours
an equally long duration. While before the 15th century it was
customary to trace the preparatory drawing directly on the plaster,
in the Quattrocento the technique of drawing cartoons
to be transferred onto the plaster through pouncing and indirect
incision became widespread.

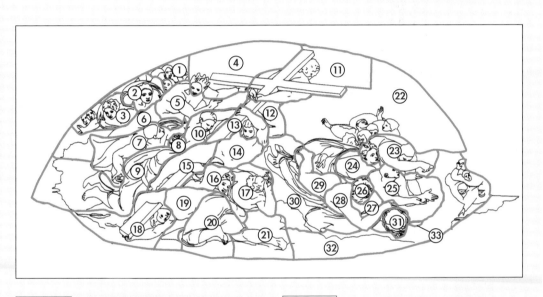

Outline of one day's work

1, 2, 3... Sequential numbers of a day's work

A diagram (for one of the lunettes of the **Last Judgement** painted many years after the ceiling) that shows Michelangelo's technique of dividing the frescoing into several day's work.

THE ANCIENT TECHNIQUE OF PREPARING COLOURS

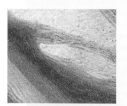

Yellow ochre, umber green, lapis lazuli, and "Sangiovanni" white, some of the colours used by Michelangelo in the Sistine Chapel.

In the *Libro dell'arte*, one of the first artistic-technical treatises in the vulgar tongue probably written at the end of the 14th century, the author Cennino Cennini explains how to prepare and use some of the basic colours that Michelangelo himself used for the frescoes in the Sistine Chapel.

Here are some significant passages from the book:

ABOUT THE NATURE OF A YELLOW COLOUR THAT IS CALLED OCHRE
Yellow of a natural colour, called ochre. This colour is found in mountain soil, where certain veins of sulphur veins can be seen. [...] It is of two kinds, light and dark. Each colour must be ground in clear water, and ground at length, so that it becomes ever more perfect. Note that this ochre is a common colour (especially when you are working with fresco) which, as I will explain, is used for flesh tones, clothing, mountains, houses, horsemen and in general for many things. And this colour is by nature greasy.

ABOUT THE NATURE OF A GREEN THAT IS CALLED UMBER GREEN
This green is a natural earth colour and is called umber green. This colour has several properties: first of all, it is an extremely greasy colour, and good to be used for faces, clothing, houses, in fresco, dry, on walls, on panels and wherever you like. Grind it in clear water; and the more you grind it the better it comes. As for tempering it, I will show you the gold bole to be used, you can put gold with this umber green. Note that the ancients used to put gold on a panel only with this green.

ABOUT THE NATURE OF "SANGIOVANNI" WHITE
White is a natural colour, but at the same time it is artificial, that is made in the following manner. Take the whitewash from the lime; put the powder in a tub for eight days, changing

the water for fresh water each day, and mix well lime and water,
so that it expels all its greasiness. Then form it into little pats,
put them in the sunshine up on the roof; and the older these pats
are the better is the white. If you want to do it quickly and well,
when the pats are dry grind them with water, and then make pats
of this and dry them again; and do so twice, and you will see how
perfect the white will be. This white is to be ground with water and
needs to be well pounded. It is good for frescoes, and without it you
can do nothing.

ABOUT THE NATURE AND THE USE OF ULTRAMARINE BLUE
Ultramarine blue is a noble colour, beautiful, perfect above all others.
[…] And if you want good stone, take the one most full of blue. […]
Pound it in a covered bronze mortar, so that it does not fly away
in dust; then put it again in your covered mortar and grind it
without water; then take a covered sieve, like the one used
by druggists to prepare spices; […] the more finely you grind it,
the more the blue comes fine […]. Then take from the druggist
six ounces of turpentine, three onces of mastic, three ounces
of new wax, for each pound of lapis lazuli; put all these things
in a new tub, and make them melt together.

(From Cennino Cennini, *Il libro dell'arte* [after 1398],
Giunti, Florence 1943, pp. 45-46, 49, 52-55).

THE SUBJECTS REPRESENTED

Isaiah
(1508-1512),
detail of the ceiling
of the Sistine Chapel,
Vatican City.

As regards the subjects, the central part of the ceiling is occupied by nine panels in which stories taken from Genesis are frescoed. Five of the nine scenes are smaller, with at the corners, in dynamic postures, pairs of male nudes (the famous *Ignudi*) holding bronze medallions with stories from the Biblical Books of Samuel and Kings. Following the logical-chronological order intrinsic to the nine episodes, rather than that in which they were painted, which would proceed from the opposite end, we find represented in the first five panels scenes from the Creation: the *Division of Light from Darkness*; the *Creation of the Stars*, the *Separation of the Waters*, the *Creation of Adam*, the *Creation of Eve*, the *Original Sin*; followed by three stories of Noah: the *Sacrifice of Noah*, the *Flood*, the *Drunkenness of Noah*.

In the side panels around the central area are instead represented – each with the name written on a plaque below held by a putto – seven *Prophets* and five *Sibyls*, they too considered, although belonging to the pagan world, among those who had announced the coming of Christ: ('Teste David cum Sibylla' recited the *Dies Irae* already in the 12ᵗʰ century).

In the vaulting cells and in the lunettes Michelangelo painted the *Ancestors of Christ* from Abraham to Joseph.

In the lateral pendentives – surmounted by bronze nudes frescoed also on the summit of the vaulting cells – are illustrated four scenes from the Old Testament, which allude to the Messianic promise: the *Bronze Serpent*, the *Chastisement of Aman*, *David and Goliath*, *Judith and Holophernes*.

THE SISTINE BEFORE MICHELANGELO

What did the Sistine Chapel look like before Michelangelo began frescoing its ceiling? The old decoration created, unlike the present one, a sober symmetric structure that allowed a horizontal reading of the hall. On three of the walls we can still today see the original frescoed bands, one above the other: at the top, beside the windows, is a succession of Popes by Fra Diamante, Ghirlandaio, Botticelli and Cosimo Rosselli; in the centre are cycles taken from the Old and New Testament (1481-1483) painted by the finest artists working at that time in Umbria and Tuscany: Perugino, Pinturicchio, Botticelli, Cosimo Rosselli, Signorelli, Bartolomeo della Gatta, Ghirlandaio and Piero di Cosimo (although the two episodes on the wall facing the altar are remakes from the late 16th century). Lastly, in the lower band, are some false hangings (over which were hung, on the occasion of solemn ceremonies, real tapestries woven to the cartoons by Raphael from 1515-1516, and thus subsequent to Michelangelo's ceiling but prior to the *Last Judgement*). What is no longer visible, and what Michelangelo saw instead in that year of 1508, is the decoration on the wall behind the altar, the lunettes above the windows, and of course the ceiling. On the wall behind the altar were two more windows flanked by figures of Popes. There were also three frescoes by Perugino, the first two stories of the cycles in the middle band and an altarpiece frescoed with the *Assumption of the Virgin* (everything later deleted by the *Last Judgement*). On the ceiling then, Pier Matteo d'Amelia had painted a simple starry sky, a sky that Michelangelo covered but surely did not darken, painting over it one of the superb masterpieces of all times.

Study of hands
(c. 1508),
London, British Museum.

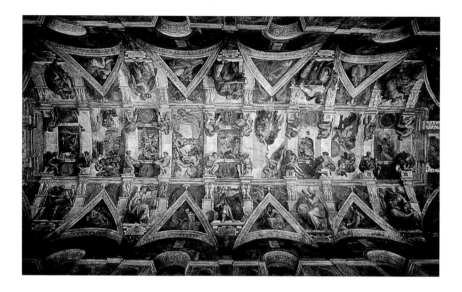

THE CEILING
OF THE SISTINE CHAPEL

'I hereby state that today, 10 May 1508, I Michelangelo the sculptor have received from His Holiness Pope Julius II five hundred ducats [...] to paint the ceiling of Pope Sisto's Chapel, on which I start to work today'. Michelangelo himself informs us of the date when he began to work on the ceiling of the Sistine Chapel. He accepted this titanic undertaking unwillingly, his mind intent on another project much more appealing to him: the Tomb of Julius II which the Pope himself had commissioned of him in 1505 but about which he had then changed his mind, giving priority to other works.

The «tragedy of the tomb», as Michelangelo was to call the beleaguered realization of the Pope's tomb, continued to be a thorn in his side for a good forty years, until 1545, amid ceaseless conflict between the sculptor, Julius II and his heirs, with continuously changing projects, work proceeding slowly and frequent interruptions. Not by chance, when in 1508 Michelangelo accepted the contract for the frescoes to be painted in the Chapel at the desire of Sixtus IV, he defiantly signed it Michelangelo "sculptor", reiterating this qualification

The ceiling
of the Sistine Chapel,
before the restoration.

in his letters from that period. The need to fresco the ceiling of the Sistine Chapel again had arisen after damage undergone by the old decoration starting from 1504, when a large crack had opened in the ceiling. Now the fact that when it was decided to repaint the ceiling the task was assigned to Michelangelo is surprising, since his fame was certainly not linked to painting, an activity in which he had engaged very little.

Bramante, one of the numerous great talents at the court of Julius II, expressed his opposition to this choice. 'I think that he [Michelangelo] has no desire to do it, since he has not drawn many figures'. Nevertheless, the Pope showed boundless faith in Michelangelo's skill, and was determined to give him the commission. In doing so the Pope, voluntarily or not, was again launching a challenge between two supreme artists, like the one where Michelangelo had recently opposed the detested Leonardo in the Palazzo della Signoria in Florence. At the same time that Michelangelo was frescoing the ceiling of the Sistine Chapel, the young Raphael was in fact working, amid general admiration, on the decoration of the "Stanze Vaticane".

A diagram of the subjects painted in the Sistine Chapel.

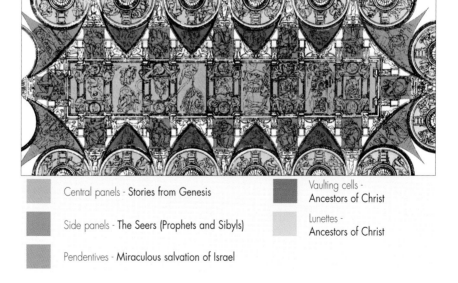

Central panels - **Stories from Genesis**

Side panels - **The Seers (Prophets and Sibyls)**

Pendentives - **Miraculous salvation of Israel**

Vaulting cells - **Ancestors of Christ**

Lunettes - **Ancestors of Christ**

The ceiling of the
Sistine Chapel,
(1508-1512),
after the restoration,
Vatican City.

But this time things were different, since Raphael considered Michelangelo a master – paying homage to him in the *School of Athens* by depicting him as Heraclitus and using the Sistine frescoes as model for other paintings in the "Stanze Vaticane" – while the Tuscan genius seemed to appreciate the young man from Urbino.

The iconographic program initially chosen for the ceiling of the Sistine Chapel was quite simple. Michelangelo was to paint the imposing figures of the Twelve Apostles in the vaulting cells and in the side pendentives, while in the center he was to limit himself to an architectural decoration.

Instead, on the immense ceiling of this hall over five hundred square meters in size, the incomparable artist's brush was to depict the history of mankind from primordial chaos to the promise of Redemption: a grandiose prologue to the coming of Christ animated by nearly three hundred and thirty-six figures, a perfect ensemble of plastic volumes and glowing colours framed by a painted architecture, appearing to open outwards and free from any strict compliance with the rules of Renaissance perspective.

In a letter from 1523 Michelangelo claims for himself merit for the whole ambitious plan, stating that since the initial project seemed to him 'a poor thing', the Pope had given him 'a new order,

that I should do what I wanted, that he would content me'.

Yet, considering the complexity and density of the allegoric and theoretic meanings expressed in the Sistine ceiling, it is hard to believe that such a cycle of frescoes could spring only from the imagination of an artist, no matter how supremely talented.

It is more likely to suppose that Michelangelo collaborated with the learned theologians of the Papal court, who would have suggested themes and ideas then developed by the artist in his own personal manner.

Study for the "Eritrean Sibyl" (1508-1512), London, British Museum.

Study for the nude above the "Persian Sibyl" (1508-1512), Haarlem, Teyler Museum.

Among the names suggested by the experts are those of the Franciscan Marco Vigerio and Egidio da Viterbo, who had been a pupil of Marsilio Ficino in Florence. And in fact a Neo-platonic interpretation of the ceiling has predominated among the critics, although a recent proposal suggests that Michelangelo's frescoes may be interpreted in relation to the preaching of Girolamo Savonarola.

Lastly, Michelangelo was to some extent limited in his design for the ceiling by the iconographic plan of the long walls below it, decorated with two bands of fresco in which, near the end of the 15th century, such artists as Botticelli, Ghirlandaio and Perugino had depicted *Stories of Moses* and *Stories of Christ*.

Evidently Michelangelo could only go further back, starting from the origin of the world. In any case, it is interesting to note that the artist's first biographers say nothing about the allegorical interpretation of Michelangelo's masterpiece, giving only descriptions, although highly detailed.

Michelangelo completed the titanic initiative of the ceiling within four years. Tradition has it that the artist trusted only his own forces, working alone, in perfect solitude, with no assistance.

In reality, the restoration carried out in the late 1980s has revealed a minimum collaboration by assistants, basically involving the first three stories in the central panels (those of Noah) and secondary elements such as medallions, reliefs on the throne and decorative elements. Everything was done, however, under the strict, direct control of Michelangelo who did not leave to his assistants the wide margin of freedom normally conceded by other famous artists of the times (such as Ghirlandaio).

In preparation for the frescoes, great importance was assigned to the making of cartoons (all lost), executed with the greatest care and precision for almost every figure.

On the first half of the ceiling the cartoons were transposed with the pouncing technique, except for one or two characters; on the second half – although pouncing was still used for some parts – in the main scenes incision was always used (except for the *Creation of Adam* where both techniques were employed), a method that calls for faster, more "extemporaneous" fresco painting. As the work proceeded, from the door of the chapel towards the altar, the artist's style gradually matured, achieving greater structural monumentality and increased luminosity in the stories of the second part of the ceiling.

Restoration of the ceiling has also brought to light the original colours of the frescoes, which had been darkened for centuries by dirt and soot: light, cold,

Project for the scene of "Judith and Holophernes" for the ceiling of the Sistine Chapel
(c. 1508),
Haarlem, Teyler Museum.

transparent colours, unnatural colours (totally different from those of the contemporary Venetian masters of the 16th century), colours "of the soul" already experimented in the *Doni Tondo* and anticipating the Mannerist palette.

On 15 August 1511 the ceiling was partially uncovered, after Michelangelo had frescoed the first half, on the feast of the Assumption, to which the chapel was dedicated. A year later, on 1 November 1512, All Saints' Day, it was definitively inaugurated. This is the artist's comment in a letter to his father: 'I have finished the chapel that I was painting: and the pope is very satisfied'.

Creation of Adam
(1508-1512),
detail of the ceiling
of the Sistine Chapel,
Vatican City.

MICHELANGELO'S TEMPERAMENT

Daniele da Volterra,
**Portrait of
Michelangelo**
(c. 1566),
Florence,
Accademia Gallery.

'You cannot deal with him' exclaimed Julius II complaining about the bad temper of Michelangelo, who was a very difficult man – unsociable, rude, proud, touchy and stubborn.

With the Pope, whose character was also strong and irascible, Michelangelo's relationship was stormy; he allowed himself to do and say things that no other artist would have dared, even risking, with his behaviour, a diplomatic incident between Rome and Florence. This took place in early 1506, when Michelangelo arrived in Rome with the marble he had personally chosen at Carrara for the Tomb of Julius II. Although the Pope himself had commissioned this project, he had temporarily lost interest in it, and Michelangelo was kept waiting for a very long time by the Pope who never found time to receive him. At last the artist, enraged, sent word to His Holiness that if he wanted to see him he should come looking for him and, having said this, left for Florence. Three Papal briefs to the Florentine authorities had to be sent before Michelangelo could be persuaded to change his mind, agreeing to meet the Pope again and ask forgiveness of him. Peace between the two was finally made in November of that same year 1506 in Bologna, where Julius II had triumphantly entered the city, defeating the Bentivoglio Signoria, but this episode shows how difficult dealing with Michelangelo could be, even for a Pope.

His vocation of solitary, isolated man and artist places him within that group of artists classified by the scholar Rudolf Wittkower as "born under Saturn", influenced by the planet that seems to govern melancholy and extravagant temperaments. For Michelangelo, the price of being a genius was probably a life of loneliness and suffering: 'I stay here in misery and with great pain, and I have no friends of any kind and I do not want any, and I have not got enough time to eat as much as I need', wrote the artist to his brother Buonarroto in 1509, a year after beginning work on the Sistine ceiling. Unsightly and shabby in his appearance and life-style, with very few friends and so heedless of manner as to appear insolent, Michelangelo worked without pause, absorbed by creative frenzy. When working he even forgot to eat and sleep, often going on working during the night, painting by the light of a candle inserted in a paper cap: an ingenious device that curiously links him to another "deviant" genius who lived many years later: Van Gogh, who used this device and improved it to paint his extraordinary nocturnal paintings. Genius and desperation seem universal and timeless.

I o gia facto un gozo in questo stento
chome fa lacqua a gacti in lombardia
over da levo paese chessi sisia
cha forza luentre apicha socto lmento
La barba al cielo ella memoria sento
in sullo scrignio elpecto fo darpia
elpennel sopral uiso tuctavia
mel fa gocciando un richo pavimento
E lombi entrati miso nella peccia
e fo delcul p chontrapeso groppa
e passi senza gliochi muovo invano
Dinanzi misallunga lachoraccia
ep piegarsi adietro si ragroppa
e tendomi chomarcho soriano
po fallace e strano
surgie il iudicio che lamente porta
che mal sitra p cerboctana torta
la mia pictura morta
di fendi orma giovanni el mio onore
non sendo in loco bo ne io pictore

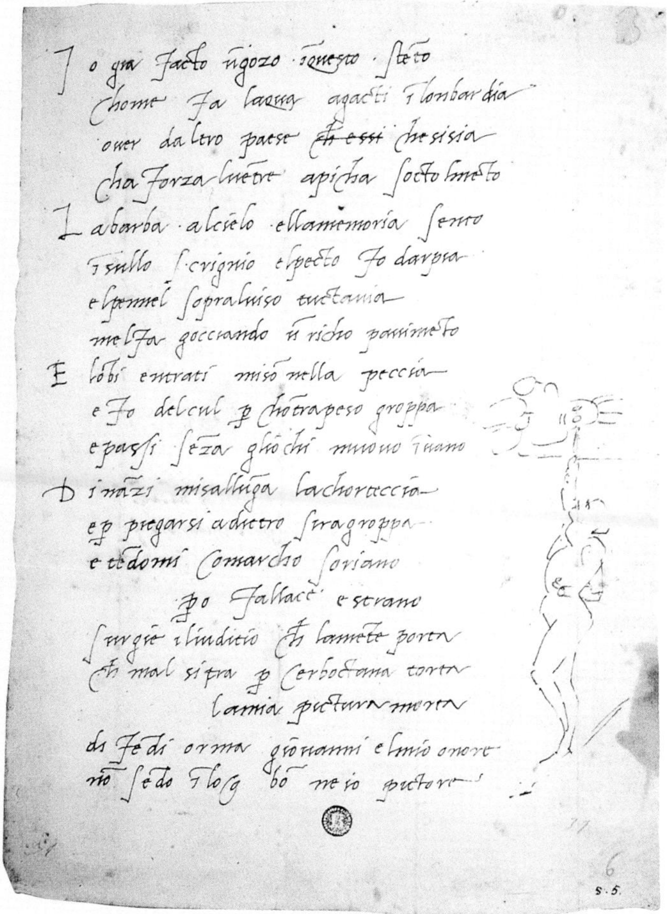

Sheet with a sonnet by Michelangelo in which he sketches himself painting the Sistine ceiling (1511-1512), Florence, Casa Buonarroti.

1513/1534 The last Florentine years

THE MEDICEAN CHAPELS AND THE "CAPTIVES"

With the new Pope Leo X, the former Giovanni de' Medici, Michelangelo Buonarroti went back to work in Florence, where in 1512, a year before the election of Lorenzo the Magnificent's son to the papal throne, the Pope's family had returned to power, bringing to an end the Republican interlude.

It was obvious that Pope Leo should be particularly attentive to his native city, especially because it was necessary to emphasize the return of the Medici family to Florence, reasserting its prestige. Michelangelo had until now been a sculptor and then a painter against his will. Under the Medici Pope he turned for the first time to architecture as well, confirming himself as an eclectic artist, in accordance with that figure of "complete" artist typical of the Renaissance with its supremely talented personalities such as Leonardo, Raphael or, although on a more modest level, Giorgio Vasari. The first commission assigned by the Pope to Michelangelo was for the completion of the San Lorenzo façade which had been left in the rough stage.

It was the "family" church, always patronized by the Medicis, as it was located in "their" quarter, the area extending around the splendid residence that Cosimo the Elder had commissioned Michelozzo to design and build.

This first task, assigned in 1518, was never carried out and the façade remains unfinished still today, although striking in its majestic simplicity. Michelangelo's project has survived in a wooden model now in the Florentine museum-house of the artist, although the statues that were to decorate it, twelve imposing marble figures, six bronze sculptures and seven large reliefs, are missing.

This first task having been left unfulfilled, in 1520 Leo X, assisted by Cardinal Giulio de' Medici – who was in turn to become Pope in 1523 under the name of Clement VII – again insisted on the San Lorenzo complex, requesting the artist to build within the church a new family chapel modelled on the first mausoleum-chapel annexed by the Medici to the building, that Old Sacristy designed by Filippo Brunelleschi between 1421 and 1426.

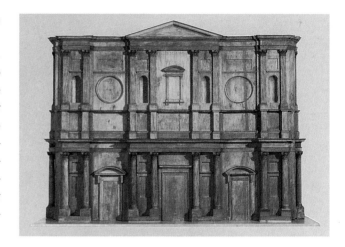

Wooden model for the façade of San Lorenzo in Florence (c. 1519), Florence, Casa Buonarroti.

Bartolomeo Ammannati, Grand staircase of the Laurentian Library in Florence (1559), to the project by Michelangelo.

View of the New Sacristy, Florence, San Lorenzo, Medicean Chapels.

Tomb of Giuliano
de' Medici,
Duke of Nemours
(1526-1531)
Florence, San Lorenzo,
New Sacristy,
Medicean Chapels.

Tomb of Lorenzo
de' Medici,
Duke of Urbino
(1525-1527)
Florence, San Lorenzo,
New Sacristy,
Medicean Chapels.

Just as Filippo Brunelleschi's Sacristy had housed – in a space decorated by such artists as Donatello and Verrocchio – the remains of Giovanni di Bicci, Cosimo the Elder's father, and the latter's sons, Piero and Giovanni de' Medici, so the chapel now commissioned of Michelangelo was to hold the tombs of Lorenzo the Magnificent and his brother Giuliano as well as those of the younger members of the Medici family who had died recently or prematurely: Giuliano Duke of Nemours (son of the Magnificent and brother of Leo X) and Lorenzo Duke of Urbino (the Pope's nephew).

From the new Florentine commission sprang one of Michelangelo's superlative works, the New Sacristy of San Lorenzo, later incorporated in the monument called the Medicean Chapels, the ensemble made up of Michelangelo's chapel and the 17th century one known as "the Princes' Chapel".

Conceived as counterpart, not only ideal but also "physical" (being located on the other side of the transept) to Brunelleschi's Old Sacristy, the New Sacristy reiterates its square structure covered by a dome and its elements in "pietra serena".

However, the interior designed by Michelangelo appears much more tense and dramatic – as compared to the older model – and presents very complex characteristics: a strikingly impressive

Detail of the statue of
Giuliano de' Medici, Duke of Nemours
(1526-1531),
Florence, San Lorenzo,
New Sacristy,
Medicean Chapels.

Detail of the statue of
Lorenzo de' Medici, Duke of Urbino
(1525-1527),
Florence, San Lorenzo,
New Sacristy,
Medicean Chapels.

interior where architecture and sculpture meet to create a place of highly enigmatic symbolism, the significance of which is still debated by the experts. As for other works by the great artist, here too a Neo-platonic interpretation seems most fitting.

In the light of this Neo-platonic interpretation the New Sacristy as a whole should be viewed as an image of the universe with the three overlapping spheres of the underworld, the world of mankind and the heavenly vault. From their tombs the souls of the dead, watched over by the allegorical figures of Time and the Rivers (the latter left unrealised) would rise to eternity, symbolised by the Madonna.

Unfortunately for posterity, only two of the tombs were completed, those of the youngest generation of the Medici family, the two dukes. In idealized rather than realistic figures, Lorenzo Duke of Urbino is portrayed in a meditative pose (Vasari called him "the Thoughtful"), while Giuliano Duke of Nemours is modelled on the statues of Roman emperors, wearing a cuirass and bearing the imperial sceptre.

On each tomb are two allegorical statues, among Michelangelo's most extraordinary works: *Night* and *Day* on Giuliano's sarcophagus; *Dusk* and *Dawn* on Lorenzo's sepulchre. Michelangelo also sculpted the beautiful *Ma-*

donna and Child placed on the opposite side of the altar.

This sculpture, flanked by the statues of the patron saints of the Medici family *Cosmas* and *Damian* (the work of two pupils, Giovanni Angelo Montorsoli and Raffaello da Montelupo), stands solemnly above the simple sarcophagus that holds the remains of Lorenzo the Magnificent and his brother Giuliano, who was murdered in the Pazzi conspiracy of 1478.

As previously mentioned, Michelangelo had also been requested to sculpt four allegorical statues of the *Rivers* to be placed on the floor, and four other figures for the niches beside the two dukes, but none of these statues was realised.

Dawn
(1525-1527),
Florence, San Lorenzo,
New Sacristy,
Medicean Chapels.

Madonna and Child
(1521-1534),
Florence, San Lorenzo,
New Sacristy,
Medicean Chapels.

Dawn
(1525-1527), detail,
Florence, San Lorenzo,
New Sacristy,
Medicean Chapels.

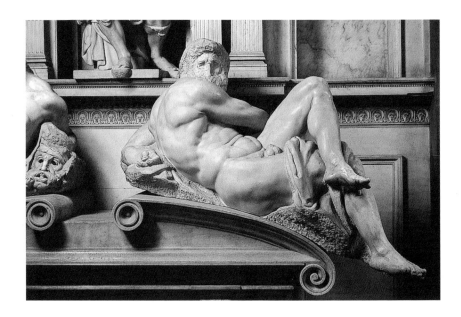

Day
(1526-1531),
Florence, San Lorenzo,
New Sacristy,
Medicean Chapels.

The project remained unfinished both for political reasons (the Medici were exiled again and the Republic was restored in Florence subsequent to the Sack of Rome in 1527) and for the personal vicissitudes of the artist, who definitively left for Rome in 1534. The task of completing the chapel was then assigned to Giorgio Vasari and Bartolomeo Ammannati, who worked on it from 1554 to 1555.

In 1519, a year before starting work on the New Sacristy of San Lorenzo, Michelangelo had begun to sculpt the statues of the four *Captives*. They were destined to that interminable project, the Tomb of Julius II, for which a new contract with some major changes had been stipulated in 1516.

Due to the enormous commitments taken on by the artist in this period, the sculptures remained in the rough stage, much less highly finished than the two statues made for the same tomb, the splendid *Slaves* now in the Louvre.

But the fascination of the non-finished – intentional or not – that incompleteness which fully reflects Michelangelo's idea of sculpture as a process of freeing form from matter, of extracting an idea already existing in the block of marble, emanates imperiously from the

Night
(1526-1531),
Florence, San Lorenzo,
New Sacristy,
Medicean Chapels.

nude *Captives* emerging from the stone as if it held them imprisoned.

When Michelangelo died in 1564, the *Captives* were in the artist's studio in Florence, in Via Mozza. His nephew Leonardo donated them to Grand Duke Cosimo I de' Medici. Later, in 1586, the statues were placed in the garden of the Pitti Palace – the Boboli Gardens – in a highly evocative setting: the Grotto built by Bernardo Buontalenti between 1584 and 1587. There they stood until 1908, when, for obvious reasons of conservation, they were removed and replaced with moulds. They are now exhibited at the Accademia Gallery in Florence.

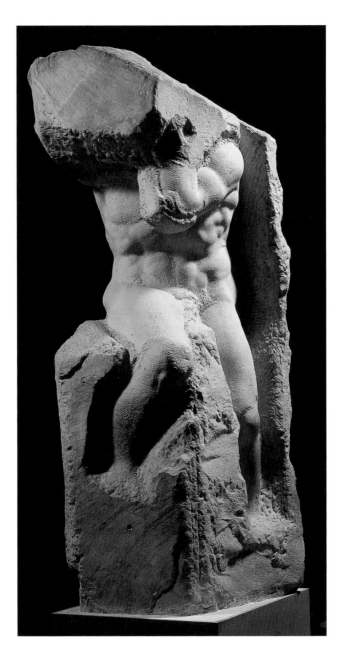

**Captive:
Atlas**
(1519-1530),
Florence,
Accademia Gallery.

Captive:
Bearded Slave
(1519-1530),
Florence,
Accademia Gallery.

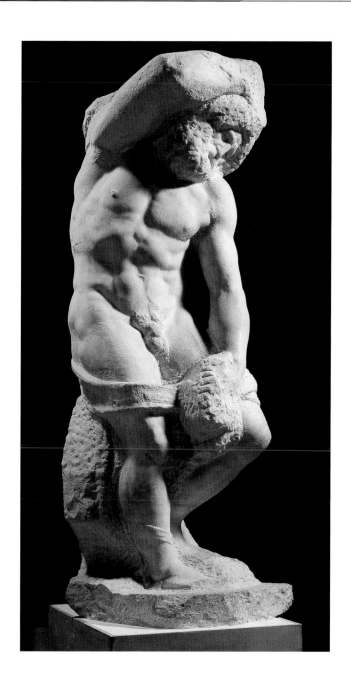

Captive:
Young Slave
(1519-1530),
Florence,
Accademia Gallery.

Captive:
Awakening Slave
(1519-1530),
Florence,
Accademia Gallery.

MICHELANGELO AND MANNERISM

The influence of Michelangelo on the artists of his time was enormous. The determinant role of his works in the development of Mannerism, the foremost artistic current of the mid-15th century in Italy, is probably the greatest heritage left by Michelangelo, who had no important direct pupils. In the Lives – whose first edition dates from 1550, when Michelangelo, seventy-five years old, was beginning to sculpt the *Bandini Pietà* – Giorgio Vasari proclaims the absolute supremacy of the genius from Caprese, with whom art had reached its highest peak. Leonardo da Vinci, Bramante and Raphael were also deemed by Vasari the masterly interpreters of what the writer calls the "third manner", or "modern manner", intending by these expressions to indicate the style, the formal stage attained by the art of his century, the 16th. In Vasari's opinion, with the "modern manner" – after the "manner" of the first period, the 14th century and that of the second, the 15th – the arts had arrived at perfection. And because, according to the author of the *Lives*, the aim of art is to imitate nature ("mimesis") but not all artists are capable of doing this, he suggests taking as a model the works of those masters who had excelled, namely Leonardo, Bramante, Raphael and Michelangelo. These considerations form the theoretic basis for what Vasari and his school were to achieve in Florence between 1567 and 1577, under the sign of that new sensitivity summed up in the term "Mannerism". But in expressing these concepts, the eclectic 16th century artist was merely codifying a tendency that had existed for some time in the Tuscan city, which was gradually being consolidated.

Mannerism, in fact, had originated in Florence around 1520, the year of Raphael's death, conventionally taken as the date when this movement began. In Florence young artists such as Rosso Fiorentino, Pontormo and Domenico Beccafumi painted works in which the influence of the great contemporary masters, especially Michelangelo – who had returned to the city in 1516 – was strikingly evident. For the artists of the Florentine "proto-Mannerism" (commonly called the first Florentine Mannerism to distinguish it from its Roman counterpart, the current that spread throughout 16th century Italy and Europe) Michelangelo's works were a sort of gospel, a text to be diligently studied. In the case of Pontormo, the cult of Michelangelo was reinforced by the friendship that bound the two artists, and it has even been conjectured that Pontormo journeyed to Rome in 1511, when the vault of the Sistine Chapel was nearly finished. The Sistine frescoes were the

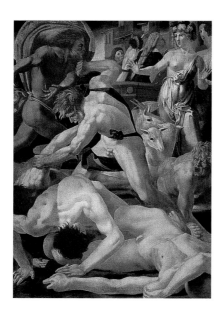

Rosso Fiorentino,
**Moses defends
Jethro's daughters**
(c. 1523),
Florence, Uffizi Gallery.

work taken as model by the Florentine Mannerists, obviously along with the *Doni Tondo*.

Already in that first crucially important panel painting Michelangelo had included some elements which were to become canonical to Mannerist art: the sinuous line described by the Virgin's movement as she twists backwards was to develop into the serpentine figure typical of Mannerist works, while the sharply contrasting colours, with their acid, iridescent tones – later used with even greater refinement in the Sistine – were also to be reiterated in Mannerist painting.

While in the *Deposition* painted by Pontormo for the Florentine church of San-

ta Felicita between 1525 and 1528 the debt to Michelangelo is obvious, among the early works of Florentine Mannerism are the Two Saints painted by the same artist, 1519-1520, for the church of his native village (Pontorme di Empoli, near Florence) and the *Marriage of the Virgin* painted by Rosso Fiorentino in 1523. Only four years after the completion of Rosso's altarpiece, the event responsible for the spread of "Mannerism" throughout Italy and all Europe occurred. In 1527 Rome, invaded by the Lansquenets of Emperor Charles V, was laid waste. This was the disastrous episode of the Sack, whose consequences included the dispersion of the artists who had admired and imitated the great masters of the early 16th century, primarily Michelangelo. In Rome, in fact, there had lived and worked, between 1520 and 1527, some of the future great interpreters of Mannerism such as Polidoro da Caravaggio, Perin del Vaga, Parmigianino, Rosso Fiorentino and Giulio Romano, who had however already settled in Mantova by 1524. Later, when the city had recovered from the crushing blow dealt by the Sack and become once more the centre of the world and of the Renaissance (in 1534 Michelangelo himself returned definitively), several late 16th century Florentine Mannerists such as Vasari, Francesco Salviati and Bronzino sojourned in Rome.

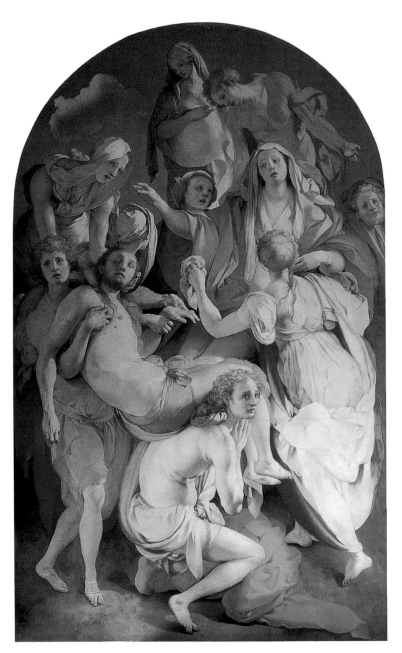

Pontormo,
Deposition
(1525-1528),
Florence,
Santa Felicita,
Capponi Chapel.

Bandini Pietà
(1550-1555),
Florence, Opera
del Duomo Museum.

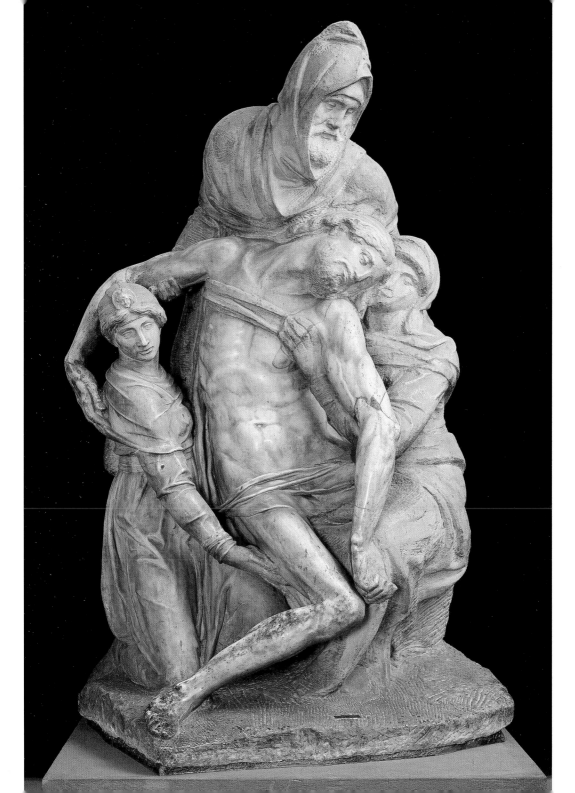

Their works were to bring back to Florence – the cradle, as has been seen, of the first Mannerism – a sort of "return" Mannerism, conscious of its Roman developments, making the Tuscan city the other basic pole, together with Rome, of the new style.

Lastly, it should be noted that the concept of "manner" was identified with Mannerism only starting from the 18th century, becoming firmly consolidated especially in the late 19th century, when the term "Mannerism" was used to indicate the post-Raphaelite artistic production of the 16th century, accused of sterile imitation of models, of virtuosity carried to an extreme, of the search for an artificial beauty and the obsessive cult of style and formal elegance.

At first, instead, the "manner" was not associated with that negative significance which was later to predominate up to our own time. For Giorgio Vasari, imitation of the great masters from the early 16th century was a highly desirable concept, a noble practice.

As always, in the 15th and 16th centuries – and that applies to all the artistic disciplines – to imitate did not mean to copy but rather to emulate a model that was the more inspiring the more perfect it was.

Brutus
(1539-1540),
Florence, Bargello
National Museum.

Genius of Victory
(1532-1534),
Florence, Palazzo Vecchio.

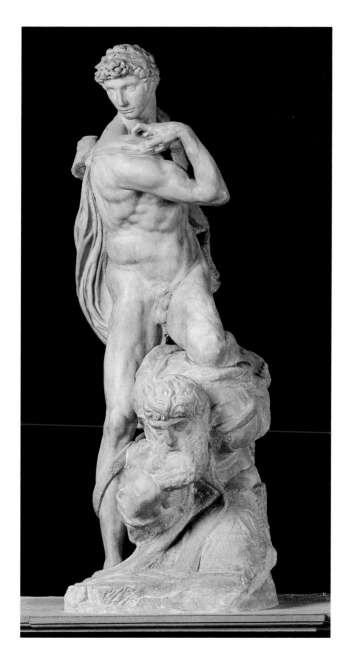

The years of the "Last Judgement"

**Conversion
of Saint Paul**
(1542-1545), detail,
Vatican City,
Pauline Chapel.

MID-16ᵀᴴ CENTURY ROME

The dramatic episode of the Sack of Rome by Imperial troops in 1527, occurring during the papacy of Clement VII, was a traumatic event not only for the city and the Pope but for the whole of Christianity, which since the Sack of Alaric, King of the Visigoths, in 410, had not witnessed such a sacrilegious attack on a city deemed almost inviolable.

After the devastating invasion by the Lansquenets of Charles V, who had laid waste the Eternal City for over nine months, sowing terror and death and causing incalculable damage, Rome still managed to rise again – also thanks to the peace between Pope and Emperor sanctioned with the King's coronation by Clement VII in 1530 – remaining a beacon of civilisation in Renaissance Europe for many years. It was clear that,

with the Sack of 1527, the dream of reinstating Rome as "caput mundi" pursued by the bellicose Julius II and by the two Medici popes, Leo X and Clement VII, was definitively shattered on the political level, showing how Italy and its small states had become mere pawns within the vaster conflict among the great foreign powers. However, it was also true that the trends that, since the early 16th century, had shifted the center of Renaissance culture from Florence to Rome, were still forcefully active, leaving to Rome its supremacy as the cultural capital of Europe. In the first place, since 1534 Michelangelo, then at the height of his fame and the acknowledged model for contemporary artists, had definitively settled in the Papal city, remaining there for thirty years until his death and painting there his masterpiece, the Sistine *Last Judgement*.

Secondly, the dispersion of almost all of the artists operating in Rome after the Sack spread throughout Italy and Europe the artistic styles developed in the Roman milieu, in particular that style (later known as the Manner or Mannerism) modelled on the three foremost figures in early 16th century Roman art: Bramante, Raphael and Michelangelo. Lastly, the fashion for collecting antiquities that had filled the papal palace and the luxurious homes of the Roman nobility with magnificent pieces continued to flourish, with collections such as that of the Farnese constantly enriched especially when, after the death of Clement VII, a member of this family became pope under the name of Paul III.

But in addition to its cultural supremacy, mid-16th century Rome remained the focal point of European attention for another reason as well: the crisis that was developing within the Catholic Church and the papacy due to the growing success of the Lutheran Reformation in the countries of Northern Europe. Rebellion against the papacy and the Roman church had broken out in early 1517, when in Wittenberg, Saxony, a German monk named Martin Luther had affixed to the cathedral door ninety-five thesis that undermined the foundations on which rested the authority of the Catholic hierarchy and doctrines. With his act Luther had voiced the general discontent felt toward the Roman Curia and its continuous oppression and demand for tribute. This was the reason for the rapid, widespread acceptance of his ideas. To the cultural ferment of 16th century Rome was thus added religious turmoil, the mobilisation of the Catholic world against the Lutheran "threat". The Roman Church began to mount a massive counterattack that was to take shape in the doctrines and provisions of the Counter-Reformation.

The first act of the Catholic response was to be the convocation of the Council of Trent, inaugurated in 1545, under the pontificate of Paul III, four years after Michelangelo – who had definitively moved to Rome in 1534 – completed the *Last Judgement* in the Sistine Chapel.

Last Judgement
(1536-1541),
Vatican City,
Sistine Chapel.

THE "LAST JUDGEMENT"

After the humiliation of the Sack of Rome, Pope Clement VII Medici came to terms with Charles V, promising to crown him Emperor in exchange for his help in restoring his family to rule in Florence. Accordingly, in 1529 the Imperial troops laid siege to the city. Michelangelo was among the defenders of the Florentine Republic, designing a number of defensive works. When in 1530 Florence, exhausted, was forced to yield and the Medici were reinstated, Michelangelo, despite his recent insubordination, was forgiven and went back to work on the Medici tombs. But either because of the despotic rule of Duke Alessandro de' Medici – later killed by his cousin Lorenzino in 1537 – or of his father's death, Michelangelo departed for Rome in 1534. This time it was a final destination; he was to stay there for thirty years more, until his death, never again returning to Florence.

When the artist arrived in Rome, Pope Clement VII had died shortly before. His successor was Cardinal Alessandro Farnese, one of the most refined man of letters and collectors of his day, whose rich collection included ancient statues such as the *Hercules* and the *Bull*, later called Farnese from his name.

Paul III, as the new pope was called, commissioned Michelangelo to carry out

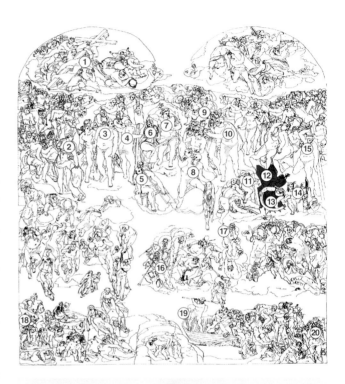

Dry additions	■ Fresco modifications

1 Archangel Gabriel (?)	11 Disma
2 Niobe (or Eva or the Church) (?)	12 Saint Blaise
3 Saint John the Baptist (or Adam)	13 Saint Catherine of Alexandria
4 Saint Andrew	14 Saint Sebastian
5 Saint Lorenz	15 Simon of Cyrene
6 The Virgin	16 The archangel Michael with the *Book of the Elect*
7 Christ the Judge	17 Proud or damned for desperation
8 Saint Bartholomew	18 Clement VII (?)
9 Saint John the Evangelist (?)	19 Charon
10 Saint Peter (or Paul III Farnese)	20 Minos (Biagio da Cesena)

Diagram of the **Last Judgement**
with the traditional identification
of characters and indication
of the modifications made
by Daniele da Volterra in 1565.

Giulio Clovio,
Last Judgement
(middle of the 16th century),
copy from Michelangelo,
Florence, Casa Buonarroti

The painting shows how
Michelangelo's fresco
looked before 1564,
when some of the naked
figures were veiled.

a project that had already existed in the plans of Clement VII Medici. It consisted of continuing the decoration of the Sistine Chapel, begun with the frescoes on the ceiling, completing it with a huge *Last Judgement* on the wall above the altar. And so in 1536, after twenty-four years, the artist resumed work in the Sistine Chapel.

The making of the new fresco called for the destruction of three works by Perugino and other figures from the existing 15th century decoration, as well as the two lunettes painted by Michelangelo himself in 1512 to conclude the decoration of the ceiling. Michelangelo illustrated the theme of the *Last Judgement* with an anthology of magnificent scenes and unforgettable figures partially inspired by the *Comedy* of Dante Alighieri.

The composition consists roughly of three bands crowned at the top by two lunettes in which wingless angels bear the symbols of Passion. In the band at the bottom of the painting are represented, on the left, the resurrection of the dead at the end of time, on the right, Hell to which Charon in his boat is ferrying the damned souls and where Minos is judging them. In the middle band, in the centre appears a group of angels with the trumpets of the Last Judgement, while on the left the Blessed rise up to the Kingdom of Heaven and on the right the Damned fall into the infernal fire.

Federico Zuccari,
**Taddeo Zuccari
copying the
"Last Judgement"
by Michelangelo**
(after 1590),
Paris, Galerie de Bayser.

Lastly, in the upper band, stands the imposing figure of Christ the Judge, flanked by the Virgin and surrounded by a host of the elect.

Compared to the traditional Italian iconography of this subject, as it had been handed down until then, the critics are unanimous in proclaiming Michelangelo's *Last Judgement* totally innovative. Not only are the figures arranged differently (especially as concerns the angels bearing the instruments of martyrdom and those with the trumpets) but the composition is not ordered in clearly distinct bands, but gives instead the impression of a whirlpool created by the raised arm of Christ, a vortex of Cyclopean figures suspended in bunches, not arranged in any precise compositional scheme. In reality, some recent studies demonstrate that the typology of the Sistine fresco falls within the Northern tradition of representing the *Last Judgement*, as shown by comparison with the painting by Rogier van der Weyden at Beaune (1443-1451), an iconographic model known to Michelangelo probably through the 14th century fresco by Buffalmacco in the Camposanto of Pisa.

The *Last Judgement* was completed in 1541. Michelangelo started to paint the fresco at the top, from the left lunette, and then proceeded downwards in orderly manner. For all the main figures a preparatory cartoon was made.

Christ the Judge
(1536-1541),
detail of the
Last Judgement,
Vatican City,
Sistine Chapel.

**Study for the
"Last Judgement"**
(c. 1533-1535),
Bayonne, Musée Bonnat.

**Study for the
"Last Judgement"**
(1533-1534),
Florence, Casa Buonarroti.

Study for the "Last Judgement" (1534), Florence, Gabinetto dei Disegni e delle Stampe, Uffizi Gallery.

At the top the cartoons were transferred by pouncing, the technique suitable to more highly refined frescoing; the lower part was instead transferred by indirect incision, having a sketchier, less elaborate effect.

Before the restoration carried out from 1990 to 1994, the surface of the fresco appeared very dirty. Restoration, bringing to light the pale, luminous colours, has been hard to accept by those accustomed to consider the *Last Judgement* a shadowy masterpiece, where the dreadfulness of the subject seemed to be expressed also through the darkness of the colours: tonalities that in the 19th century provided continuous inspiration to Romantic painters, such as Blake and Delacroix, who in his *Dante's Boat* from 1822 used murky colours inspired by the example of the Sistine *Last Judgement* as it looked at the time. Against these vivid tones uncovered by the recent cleaning operation, violent attacks were launched by critics anchored to the idea of the "dirty" Michelangelo, as it had been known for centuries.

Outstanding among the colours used by Michelangelo in the *Last Judgement* is the very expensive lapis lazuli ("ultramarine") used for the blues, the pigment responsible for that intense blue tonality of the sky so determinant to the overall effect. A substantial number of corrections, additions and dry finishing touches, sometimes made after many days' work, has also been noted.

To carry out this grandiose project Michelangelo, generally reluctant to accept any help, employed, especially in the sketching stage, one of his pupils, Urbino (Francesco Amadori), who probably also assisted – perhaps when Michelan-

Virgin (1536-1541), detail of the **Last Judgement**, Vatican City, Sistine Chapel.

gelo hurt his leg falling from a scaffolding – with some figures of the risen dead where the quality level is clearly lower. According to tradition, Michelangelo represented contemporary personalities in some figures: Saint Peter is said to display the features of Paul III; Minos those of Biagio da Cesena, against whom the artist may have sought revenge for criticism of the *Last Judgement* expressed by the master of ceremonies. Saint Bartholomew is thought to represent the writer Pietro Aretino, while on the skin of his martyrdom, which the saint holds in his hand, Michelangelo may have painted his own self-portrait. In 1545, four years after the unveiling of the *Last Judgement*, Paul III convoked the Council of Trent, an attempt by the Church of Rome to react to the advance of the Protestant Reformation, which had started with Luther's theses in 1517 and was now establishing itself among the formerly Catholic peoples of Northern Europe. Following the Council of Trent, a wave of severity swept through the countries that had remained Catholic, with the application of a series of measures based on the strictest observance of dogma.

Angels
(1536-1541),
details in the right lunette
of the **Last Judgement**
before and after
the 1994 restoration.

Among the actions taken by the Council, which closed in 1563, was censorship of the nudes in the *Last Judgement*, considered obscene. This decision dates from January 1564. Michelangelo died a month later, on 18 February. The task of covering the "scandalous" nudity of his figures was assigned to one of his friends and pupils, Daniele da Volterra. The "Braghettone", as the artist was then called because of the "braghe" (pants) with which he dressed the naked bodies painted by the master, fulfilled this task in 1565, using the fresco technique on some figures, as for

example Saint Blaise and Saint Catherine, originally naked and crouched one above the other in a position judged equivocal.

But the changes made by the "Braghettone" were not the only censorial interventions carried out on the *Last Judgement*, which continued from the late 16th century probably up to the 18th. As concerns the "braghe", the recent restoration has been rather conservative, leaving the additions by Daniele da Volterra and most of the later ones as well, according to the principle of keeping everything that has historical value.

Marcello Venusti,
Last Judgement
(1549),
copy from Michelangelo,
Naples, Capodimonte
National Museum.

THE PAULINE CHAPEL

The *Last Judgement* was not to be Michelangelo's last painting nor the last work by the artist in the Vatican. In 1542, a year after the completion of the grandiose Sistine fresco, Paul III commissioned Michelangelo to decorate the Pauline Chapel as well, only recently completed by Antonio da Sangallo. Obviously Michelangelo could not refuse, but found himself literally overloaded with work, involved contemporaneously in the never-ending project for the Tomb of Julius II and his new tasks as architect for the Farnese Pope: the renovation of the palace belonging to the Pope's family, the arrangement of the Piazza del Campidoglio and, above all,

The vault of the Pauline Chapel (1542-1550), Vatican City.

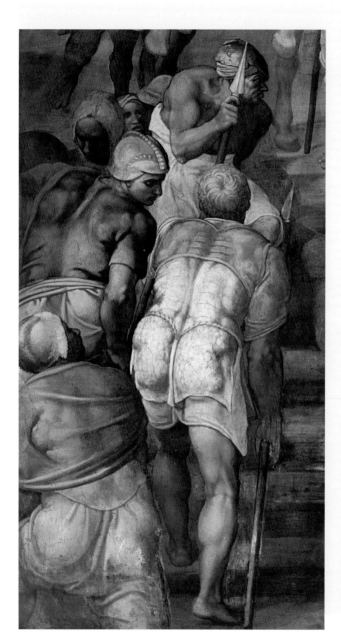

**Crucifixion
of Saint Peter**
(1542-1545),
whole and detail,
Vatican City,
Pauline Chapel.

the continuation of his work as chief architect
of Saint Peter's, a position to which he had
been appointed in 1546. It is thus
unsurprising that the frescoes in the Pauline
Chapel are not the artist's finest, considering
not only his other commitments but also
the fact that Michelangelo was already
about seventy years old. The stories painted
in the Pope's private chapel represent
the culminating episodes in the lives
of the two greatest Apostles. On one wall
is frescoed the *Conversion of Saint Paul*,
opposite it is the *Crucifixion of Saint Peter*.
An unusual note, in these two frescoes,
is struck by the presence of horses, since
in the works of Michelangelo, basically
interested in the human figure, animals
are practically absent, even from scenes
where they could have been abundantly
included, such as the *Flood* on the Sistine
ceiling, where only a donkey's muzzle
appears on the left side of the painting,
while above the ark, on which rests
the dove of Peace, only a few more
birds are wheeling.

MICHELANGELO THE ARCHITECT

Michelangelo first worked as architect in Florence. Here, besides the previously mentioned projects, he was given another important commission by Pope Clement VII Medici, the design of the Laurentian Library, again within the San Lorenzo complex. Michelangelo began this project in 1524 but in this too case the work remained uncompleted. Thanks to the use, in an interior, of outdoor elements such as windows and columns, the impression given by the entrance hall of the Laurenziana is that of being inside a courtyard enclosed by the façades of four palaces. A magnificent feature is the monumental staircase built by Bartolomeo Ammannati which dominates the centre of the entrance.

In 1534 Michelangelo, having definitively returned to Rome, became intensively engaged in architecture here as well. Besides continuing the renovation of the Farnese Pope's family palace the artist, still on behalf of Paul III, worked from 1538 on the arrangement of the Piazza del Campidoglio. This was in all aspects an urban planning initiative, the designing – for the first time in Rome – of a public space based on a detailed preliminary project. The area involved in the project covered the Capitoline hill. In the 16th century this area appeared severely degraded and of difficult access.

Porta Pia,
designed by Michelangelo
between 1560 and 1564.

Whole and detail
of Saint Peter's dome
(1546-1588/1590).

Michelangelo planned to change it by creating a space that would be as respectful as possible of the pre-existing architectural structures and that would eliminate the obstacles to reaching the hilltop. With this objective, he retained the two existing buildings, the Medieval Palazzo Senatorio and the 16th century Palazzo dei Conservatori, and designed a third, the Palazzo Nuovo (now seat of the Capitoline Museums), thus closing the square on three sides like a horseshoe. He also renovated the facades of the existing palaces and oriented the lateral buildings on slightly diverging lines, opening out from the central building (the Palazzo Senatorio). Through this theatrical perspective device – anticipatory of urban planning trends of the following century – the space appears widened, and the feeling of asymmetry deriving from a square whose length exceeds its width is substantially attenuated. At the centre, on a base also designed by Michelangelo, was placed a famous ancient statue, the equestrian monument of the Emperor Marcus Aurelius (thought at the time to portray Constantine) which Paul III Farnese had donated to the Roman Senate. Lastly, Michelangelo designed a sweeping monumental stairway departing from the centre of the open side of the square, providing comfortable access to it. The artist never saw his work carried out, since the project was completed only around the mid-17th century. In fact the paving he designed, with the pattern of a star enclosed in an oval shape, was completed only in 1940. But Michelangelo's most important work in Rome was the continuation of the restoration of Saint Peter's. Appointed chief architect of the Fabric of Saint Peter's in 1546, a role of great responsibility occupied before him by Bramante, Raphael and Antonio da Sangallo, Michelangelo retained the concept of the central plan proposed by Bramante, reiterating in it in clearer, simpler shapes. To crown the building he then designed a majestic dome inspired by the one built by Brunelleschi for the Cathedral of Florence, but of much more imposing dimensions.

Michelangelo died when the dome had been built only up to the tambour. It was completed, between 1588 and 1590, by Giacomo della Porta and Domenico Fontana, who lengthened it in shape as compared to the original version. Today the dome of Saint Peter's remains the element which more than any other bears the trace of the original project, substan-

tially modified by Carlo Maderno in the 17th century. In the last years of his life, between 1560 and 1564, Michelangelo was commissioned by Pope Pius IV to design – at the end of that Via Pia (now Via XX Settembre) built at the desire of the Pope himself – a gateway of clearly commemorative nature, also named for the new Pope: Porta Pia. In this gate, finished after the artist's death, Michelangelo used exposed brickwork, reminiscent of the ancient Roman building tradition.

Saint Peter's dome, detail.

THE LAST "PIETÀ"

That Michelangelo considered himself
basically a sculptor and felt satisfied only when he held a chisel in his hand is
well known. His love of sculpture was
stronger than ever near the end of his
life, when the artist sculpted, not on commission but for his own pleasure, some
works in which he returned to the theme
of the *Pietà*, never again confronted after the youthful exploit that had made him
famous. But now Michelangelo no longer sculpted serene, composed groups
such as the Vatican *Pietà*, but deeply
dramatic sculptures, in which the recur-
ring thought of impending death, obses-
sively reiterated, is clearly evident.

These last *Pietà* are plainly the arrival
point of an artist and a man now old
and rich in experience, who meditates
upon a theme felt to be the central issue
in his life. And this not merely for his ad-
vanced age but also for a growing religious turmoil which seems to reflect the
crisis of the Catholic Church after the
shock of the Lutheran Reformation, the
anxieties of a new spirituality that was
spreading within the Catholic world,
even after the convocation of the Council of Trent and the launching of the
Counter-Reformation. And it is revealing that the only woman Michelangelo
frequented, whom he considered his
spiritual guide, the muse to whom he

**Resurrection
of Christ**
(1532), detail,
London, British Museum.

donated drawings and sonnets, with whom he engaged in erudite discussions and exchanged letters, was Vittoria Colonna. Around this highly cultured Roman noblewoman, in fact, had gathered a group of friends belonging to Catholic "reformist" circles, where the renewal of the Roman Church was discussed: personages such as Sadoleto, Carafa, Thiene, Cardinal Reginald Pole and others, all profoundly influenced by the Spanish Juan Valdés, who had disseminated reformist concepts in Italy, bearing the message of Erasmus and of Luther. The *Pietà* sculpted by Michelangelo in his last years follow one another in a crescendo of "non-finito". This corresponds, as in some of the sculptor's previous works, to a precise stylistic and expressive choice, not resulting from accident, although in the case of the *Rondanini Pietà* the problem of the "non-finished" is indubitably more complex, since the artist died while working on it. Between 1550 and 1555 Michelangelo sculpted the so-called *Bandini Pietà* (named for Francesco Bandini, who owned it until the late 17th century), now in the Opera del Duomo Museum of Florence (see p. 121). According to Vasari, Michelangelo had first decided to destine the sculpture to his own tomb, which he wished to have placed in Santa Maria Maggiore in Rome (the artist was instead buried in Santa Croce

in Florence, his corpse having been stolen away by his nephew Leonardo). The personage of Nicodemus, the hooded figure supporting Christ, is traditionally considered to be a self-portrait of Michelangelo. The work was purposely damaged by the sculptor who, unsatisfied with it, broke off the Redeemer's left arm with the blow of a hammer. Later one of his pupils, Tiberio Calcagni, reattached the broken arm and completed the group, sculpting entirely the figure of the Magdalene, but leaving unfinished the left leg of the Christ, which remained mutilated.

The *Pietà from Palestrina* takes its name from the place in which the work was found before it was moved to its present location, the Accademia Gallery in Florence. The authenticity of this group from around 1555 is now highly debated by the critics, many of whom believe that Michelangelo only roughed out the statue, which was then completed by others. On the last of the series, the touching *Rondanini Pietà*, Michelangelo worked until the evening before that 18 February 1564 on which he died – an almost incredible fact, considering that the artist was then eighty-nine years old. The group is listed in the inventory of his Roman home (now destroyed) in Macel de' Corvi, near the ruins of Trajan's Forum: 'Another statue begun for a Christ and another figure above it, linked

Pietà from Palestrina
(c. 1555),
attributed to Michelangelo or to one of his pupils,
Florence,
Accademia Gallery.

together, roughed out and not finished', are the words with which it is described in the list of his possessions. The sculpture, a work amazingly consonant with modern taste, now in the Castello Sforzesco in Milan, owes its name to its place of origin, Palazzo Rondanini in Rome. Michelangelo worked on it in stages, as proven by the numerous corrections and even radical modifications, whose most evident trace is the surviving stump of Christ's right arm, left beside the new figures; the shape and size of the arm seem to indicate a first version, dating from around 1552-1553, in which the bodies were not so emaciated but probably had more "classic" proportions.

In the second version, begun in 1554, the slenderness of the figures and the "non-finished" aspect confer on the group great dramatic force and intense spirituality. In the extreme abandon of the dead Christ's body, in the evident effort of the Virgin to support him, there exists no longer that serene composure, that harmony emanating from the *Vatican Pietà*, but grief and desperation reign supreme. But not this alone; the pathos of the *Rondanini Pietà* is even more poignant since it is mingled with tenderness, the affectionate gesture of a mother who seems almost to gather to herself and enfold, in a last desperate effort to protect him, that son whom

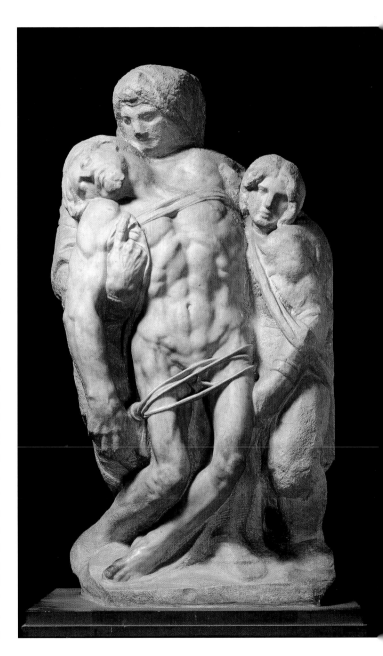

Michelangelo has portrayed as if sunken into the Virgin's body.

The iconography of these *Pietà* from the artist's late production deserves mention. While in the Vatican *Pietà* Michelangelo had used a traditional iconography, with the body of Christ lying across his mother's knees and almost cradled by the Virgin, in the *Pietà* from his late years the sculptor represented the dead body of Christ in a vertical position, sinking with all its weight and supported with visible effort. The model from which Michelangelo drew inspiration was probably that of the *Pietà* painted by Giovanni Bellini and Mantegna, where Christ's body appears almost elevated as in the Mass. But in the *Rondanini Pietà* there is a further component: the accentuated verticality of the group and the extreme thinness of the figures seem to recall medieval plastic models, especially Gothic ones, which the artist may have intended to evoke.

Rondanini Pietà (1552-1564), left unfinished in the master's house in Rome after his death, Milan, Castello Sforzesco.

MICHELANGELO THE POET

The feelings and the thought of Michelangelo also found expression, throughout his long life, in poetry and in the many letters addressed to relatives and friends. Although not a man of letters and not intending to publish his poems, Michelangelo left a number of Petrarchian sonnets in keeping with the taste of the times, where the 14th century poet was considered the supreme master of lyric poetry, as stated by Pietro Bembo in one of his 16th century treatises. But Michelangelo's verses were neither harmonious nor light, as was usually the case with the imitators of Petrarch, but imbued with formal and conceptual severity, obscurity and harshness which have for years discouraged critics and readers of this great artist's poetry. In Michelangelo's poetry artistic and aesthetic considerations, references to his lonely, fatiguing craft often appear (but at times the tone is ironic, as in the verses where the artist describes himself grappling with the frescoes of the Sistine ceiling – a situation illustrated in a self-portrait sketched in the margin of a letter – with the colours dripping into his eyes: 'My beard points skyward, I feel a hump on my nape, I have a Harpy's breast and still the paintbrush above my face makes, dripping, a brightly decorated floor'. Many are the love sonnets, including those dedicated to Tommaso Cavalieri, the handsome young man dearly beloved by the artist, inspiring him to express emotions often censured in the old editions of his poetry. As the years passed a growing anxiety and torment emerged, as in the figurative works, and it was expressly in the poetry of his maturity and old age that Michelangelo reached the highest, most touching moments of his lyricism, as in the following sonnet:

Laden with years and full of sins
and with sad habit deep-rooted and strong,
I see myself close to one and
                              [to the other death
and nourish my heart with poison.

Nor have I force enough
to change life, love, habit or destiny,
without your aid, divine and clear,
guide and restraint of any faulty course.

My dear Lord, it is not enough that
                              [you induce me
to seek the sky only so that the soul may be,
not as before, of nothing, created

Before you strip me of my mortal spoils
I pray you halve the steep, long way
and make the path more clear and sure.

Topographic index

Michelangelo's birthplace
in Caprese (Arezzo).

Casa Buonarroti
in Florence
in an old print.

Giorgio Vasari,
The tomb of Michelangelo
(1570),
Florence, Santa Croce.

Chronology

1475 On 6 March Michelangelo Buonarroti is born in Caprese (Arezzo), the second son of the Magistrate Lodovico di Leonardo di Buonarroti Simoni and Francesca, daughter of Neri di Miniato del Sera and Bonda Rucellai. His parents soon move to Florence and Michelangelo is put to nurse in Settignano.

The Pazzi Conspiracy against the Medicean Signoria, instigated by Pope Sixtus IV, fails; in the Florence Cathedral Giuliano de' Medici, brother of Lorenzo the Magnificent, is killed; Lorenzo escapes assassination.

1478

Leonardo begins the *Adoration of the Magi,* Sandro Botticelli begins the *Primavera* (completed 1482).

1481 His mother dies. First lessons at the grammar school. Meets the painter Francesco Granacci who encourages him to draw.

Botticelli begins the *Birth of Venus* (completed 1484). The paintings in the Sistine Chapel in the Vatican, where Perugino and Botticelli were the foremost artists, are completed.

1482

Raphael is born in Urbino, Leonardo signs the contract for *Virgin of the Rocks.*

1483

Innocent VIII (Giovanni Battista Cybo) is elected Pope.

1484

Ghirlandaio and his assistants begin decorating the chancel of Santa Maria Novella (completed 1490).

1486

Andrea del Verrocchio, the Florentine sculptor, dies in Venice.

1488 In Florence Michelangelo is apprenticed to Ghirlandaio's workshop for one year.

1489 He frequents the Garden of the San Marco Monastery, owned by the Medici, where he studies the collection of ancient and modern statuary.

In Florence Lorenzo de' Medici, the Magnificent, dies. Alexander VI (of the Borgia family) is elected Pope. Christopher Columbus discovers America. Piero della Francesca dies.

1492 His earliest works date from this period: the *Battle of the Centaurs,* the wooden *Crucifix* for Santo Spirito and the *Madonna of the Stairs.*

Charles VIII of France attacks Florence: Piero de' Medici, driven out of Florence, is a guest of the Bentivoglio family in Bologna. A Republic is proclaimed in Florence. Savonarola's preachings gain popular support.

1494 Flees to Venice before Charles VIII enters Florence; later moves to Bologna where he sculpts a *Kneeling Angel* for the Tomb of Saint Dominic.

Leonardo begins the *Last Supper.* In Florence Perugino opens a flourishing workshop.

1495 Returns to Florence where he sculpts small sculptures (now lost) for Lorenzo di Pierfrancesco de' Medici.

1496 Visits Rome as guest of Cardinal Riario. Sculpts a *Sleeping Cupid* (lost) and a *Bacchus* (Florence, Bargello).

Under pressure from Alexander VI, Savonarola is tried and burnt at the stake in Piazza della Signoria in Florence, on 23 May. Antonio del Pollaiolo dies in Rome.

1498 Signs a contract with the French Cardinal Jean Bilhères to sculpt a *Pietà* for Saint Peter's in the Vatican. The work is to be completed within a year for a stipulated price of 450 ducats.

Luca Signorelli begins the frescoes in the San Brizio Chapel, Orvieto Cathedral.

1499 The client of the *Pietà,* just finished, dies on 6 August.

Louis XII of France invades the Italian peninsula. The Sforza are driven out of Milan. Leonardo returns to Florence. Bramante is working in Rome. Botticelli paints the *Mystic Nativity*.

1500 Begins an altarpiece in the church of Sant'Agostino, Rome. The work may be the *Burial of Christ* (London, National Gallery), but the attribution is uncertain.

Raphael produces his first works at Città di Castello.

1501 Returned to Florence, on 5 June he is commissioned 15 sculptures for the Piccolomini altar in the Siena Cathedral. On 16 August the Florentine Republic commissions him to sculpt the *David*.

Pier Soderini becomes Gonfalonier of the Florentine Republic for life.

1502 On 12 August Florence commissions him to sculpt a second bronze *David* for Cardinal de Rohan. The work will later be completed by Benedetto da Rovezzano.

Alexander VI dies suddenly. After the brief papacy of Pius III (Piccolomini), Julius II (Della Rovere), an opponent of Alexander's policy, is elected pope. Collapse of the state of Cesare Borgia, son of Alexander VI. Leonardo begins the *Battle of Anghiari* (Florence, Salone dei Cinquecento).

1503 On 24 April the Opera del Duomo commissions 12 statues of Apostles for the interior of the Cathedral. Only *Saint Matthew* is roughed out. On 14 December the Flemish cloth merchant Alexandre Moscrou pays him 50 ducats for the *Bruges Madonna*. He sculpts the *Taddei Tondo* and the *Pitti Tondo*.

Raphael moves to Florence. With the Treaty of Blois, the Kingdom of Naples falls under Spanish rule.

1504 Soderini commissions the *Battle of Cascina* for the Salone dei Cinquecento in Palazzo della Signoria. He completes the *Bruges Madonna*. On 8 September the *David* is brought to Piazza della Signoria.

Bramante begins work on the Tempietto of San Pietro in Montorio and the Cortile del Belvedere.

1505 In March Pope Julius II commissions him to sculpt his tomb for Saint Peter's Cathedral, later placed in San Pietro in Vincoli. Michelangelo goes to Carrara to choose the marble.

Julius II defeats Bologna. The *Laocoon* is discovered in Rome. Bramante begins to build the new church of Saint Peter's. Leonardo departs for Milan.

1506 Because of conflict with the Pope, Michelangelo escapes to Florence. On 21 November he is reconciled with the Pope who requests him to sculpt a bronze statue of himself.

Raphael paints the *Baglioni Altarpiece*.

1507 Probably the year in which *Holy Family* (*Doni Tondo*) was painted for Agnolo Doni.

The League of Cambrai: Julius II, Maximilian of Hapsburg, Louis XII and Ferdinand the Catholic join forces against Venice.

1508 The monument to Julius II above the San Petronio portal is inaugurated in Bologna. Michelangelo returns to Florence where Pier Soderini commissions him to sculpt a *Hercules and Cacus*. On 10 May he accepts the task of frescoing the ceiling of the Sistine Chapel, in Rome.

The defeat of Venice. Baldassarre Peruzzi designs the Villa Farnesina for Agostino Chigi. In Rome Raphael begins work on the "Stanze" (the Vatican apartments of Julius II).

1509

The Holy League against France. Sebastiano del Piombo is in Rome. Andrea del Sarto begins the scenes from the *Life of the Virgin* in the Cloister of SS. Annunziata.

1511 On 14 or 15 August Julius II visits the Sistine Chapel, which is still unfinished.

The Medici family return to Florence. In Siena Beccafumi paints the *Trinity Triptych*, in Florence Fra Bartolomeo paints the *Mystic marriage of Saint Catherine*.

1512 The Sistine Chapel is re-opened on 31 October, the frescoes having been completed 20 days earlier.

1513 Julius II dies, succeeded by Giovanni de' Medici (Lorenzo the Magnificent's son) who takes the name of Leo X. Leonardo is in Rome.

1513 At the death of Julius II, Michelangelo signs a new contract for his tomb with the Pope's heirs: he sculpts the *Moses* and the two *Slaves* (Louvre).

1514 Bramante dies. Raphael is chief architect of Saint Peter's; he paints the *Sibyls* in the Chigi Chapel in Santa Maria della Pace in Rome and begins to decorate the "Stanza dell'Incendio di Borgo".

1514 He is commissioned to sculpt a *Risen Christ* for Santa Maria sopra Minerva. The papal chapel in Castel Sant'Angelo is built to his design.

1515 Francis I becomes King of France. With the victory of Marignano he retakes Milan. Raphael draws the cartoons for the tapestries in the Sistine Chapel. Machiavelli finishes writing *The Prince*. Andrea del Sarto begins the *Scenes from the life of John the Baptist*.

1515 In April he returns to Florence, remaining there until 1534.

1516 Charles of Hapsburg succeeds Ferdinand the Catholic as King of Spain. Ludovico Ariosto finishes the *Orlando Furioso*. Sebastiano del Piombo works on the *Deposition* (Hermitage).

1516 Another contract is drawn up for the Tomb of Julius II. Leo X commissions him to design the façade of San Lorenzo in Florence.

1517 Martin Luther launches the Protestant Reformation in Germany. Raphael and his assistants works on the "Psyche Loggia" in the Farnesina Villa and on the Vatican Loggias. Leonardo goes to France.

1517 He begins the *Captives* (Florence, Accademia Gallery).

1519 Charles V of Hapsburg is elected Emperor of the Holy Roman Empire. Leonardo dies at Amboise. In Parma Correggio paints the "Camera della Badessa" in the San Paolo Convent. Pontormo begins the frescoes in the Medici Villa, Poggio a Caiano.

1519 Leo X commissions him to design the New Sacristy in San Lorenzo, destined to house six Medici tombs. He works on the *Captives*.

1520 Raphael dies. Luther is excommunicated with the papal bull *Exurge Domine*.

1520 The Pope reduces to two the statues for the Tomb in San Lorenzo.

1521 In the Vatican, Giulio Romano frescoes the "Sala di Costantino" and Perin del Vaga the "Sala dei Pontefici".

1521 He works on the Medici tombs. In August the *Risen Christ* is placed in Santa Maria sopra Minerva in Rome.

1522 Leo X dies and is succeeded by Adrian of Utrecht. The Diet of Worms banishes Lutheranism.

1522

1523 Adrian VI dies and is succeeded by Clement VII (Giuliano de' Medici). *Scenes from the Passion* by Pontormo.

1523

1524 Giulio Romano moves to Mantova at the service of Federico Gonzaga. In Mantova work begins on Palazzo Te. Parmigianino is in Rome.

1524 Work is begun on the Laurentian Library and the statues of *Dawn* and *Dusk* for the Tomb of Lorenzo de' Medici, Duke of Urbino.

1525 Francis I of France is defeated at Pavia by Charles V. Pontormo begins the frescoes in Santa Felicita (Florence).

1525

1526 The League of Cognac against Charles V. The *Deposition of Santa Felicita* by Pontormo.

1526 He begins work on the Tomb of Giuliano, Duke of Nemours, with the sculptures of *Night* and *Day*.

1527 The Sack of Rome by the imperial Lansquenets: Jacopo Sansovino and Pietro Aretino flee to Venice.

1527 Following the expulsion of the Medici, work on the New Sacristy in San Lorenzo comes to a halt.

1530 In Bologna, Clement VII crowns Charles V, King of Italy, in return he promises to restore the Medici to power.

1530 Paints a *Leda and the Swan* for the Duke of Ferrara. Works on the Laurentian Library and the New Sacristy.

Alessandro de' Medici returns to Florence after the republican interlude.

Clement VII dies and is succeeded by Paul III (Alessandro Farnese). Ignatius of Loyola founds the Company of Jesus.

Calvin's reform in Geneva. Pietro Aretino publishes the *Ragionamenti*.

Salviati and Jacopino del Conte work on the Oratory of San Giovanni Decollato.

Benvenuto Cellini works in the service of Francis I in France.

Daniele da Volterra is commissioned to paint the *Deposition* (Trinità dei Monti).

The Holy Office is established in Rome. Cardinal Contarini, leader of the Catholic reform movement, dies.

Inaugural session of the Council of Trent: the beginning of the Counter-Reformation. Titian visits Rome.

Antonio da Sangallo the Younger dies. Giulio Romano dies in Mantua. Vasari paints the "Sala dei 100 giorni" in Palazzo della Cancelleria. Martin Luther dies.

Henry II is king of France. Charles V defeats the League of the protestant princes. Tintoretto paints the *Last Supper*.

Paul III dies and is succeeded by Julius III. First edition of the *Lives* by Giorgio Vasari.

Henry II goes to war with Charles V.

The Council of Trent ends.

Peace of Augsburg: Charles V abdicates. Julius III dies: he is succeeded by Paul IV (Giovan Pietro Carafa).

Paul IV dies and is succeeded by Pius IV, uncle of Carlo Borromeo.

The Accademia del Disegno opens in Florence on 31 January.

Daniele da Volterra, called the "Braghettone", is commissioned to cover up the parts of the *Last Judgement* deemed obscene by the Congregation of the Council of Trent.

1531 Draws the cartoons for the *Noli me tangere* (painted by Pontormo).

1534 Finishes the *Genius of Victory*. He leaves Florence for Rome, to plan work on the *Last Judgement*.

1536 He begins the *Last Judgement* on the end wall of the Sistine Chapel.

1538 Arranges the equestrian statue of *Marcus Aurelius* on the Campidoglio.

1540 He completes the bust of *Brutus* begun for Cardinal Ridolfi in 1539.

1541 The *Last Judgement* is unveiled on 31 October.

1542 The final contract for the Tomb of Julius II. Begins the frescoes in the Pauline Chapel.

1545 The statues for the Tomb of Julius II are put in place. He completes the *Conversion of Saint Paul* (Pauline Chapel).

1546 Begins the *Crucifixion of Saint Peter* (Pauline Chapel). Appointed architect of Saint Peter's, he begins to design the dome. Completes Palazzo Farnese.

1547 Begins the *Rondanini Pietà*. Vittoria Colonna, his friend and correspondent, dies.

1550 Completes the frescoes in the Pauline Chapel in Rome and begins the *Bandini Pietà*.

1552 Completes the stairway to the Campidoglio.

1553 He works on the *Bandini Pietà* (Florence, Cathedral).

1555 Pope Paul IV confirms his appointment as architect of Saint Peter's.

1556 He leaves Rome and goes to Spoleto.

1559 Sends a model for the stairway of the Laurentian Library to Florence. Probably begins the *Rondanini Pietà*.

1560 For Caterina de' Medici, designs a monument to Henry II of France. Designs the Tomb of Giangiacomo dei Medici di Marignano for the Milan Cathedral. Drawings for Porta Pia.

1563 He is appointed "chief" of the Accademia del Disegno of Florence, together with Cosimo I de' Medici.

1564 On 18 February he dies in Rome, in his home near the Trajan Forum, leaving uncompleted the *Rondanini Pietà*.

Index

The numbers in **bold** refer to the illustrations

Bibliography

Sources andmonographs:

The best editions of the biographies of Michelangelo written by his contemporaries, Vasari (1550 and 1568) and Ascanio Condivi (1553) are: G. Vasari, *La vita di Michelangelo nelle redazioni del 1550 e 1568*, edited by P. Barocchi, Milan-Naples 1962, 5 vol.; G. Vasari, *Le vite de' più eccellenti pittori, scultori et architettori... di nuovo ampliate*, Florence 1568; ed. in *Le opere di Giorgio Vasari*, edited by G. Milanesi, Florence 1878-1885, 9 vol., I-VII, 1878-1881; G. Vasari, *Le vite de' più eccellenti pittori, scultori et architettori nelle redazioni del 1550 e 1568*, Florence 1550 and 1568; edited by R. Bettarini and P. Barocchi, Florence 1966-1987, 6 vol. (of the *Lives* only); A. Condivi, *Vita di Michelangelo Buonarroti*, Rome 1553, edited by G. Nencioni, with essays by M. Hirst and C. Elam, Florence 1998.

Among the monographs: Ch. De Tolnay, *Michelangelo*, 1945-1960; H. von Einem, *Michelangelo*, Berlin 1973; R. Clements, *Michelangelo. Le idee sull'arte*, Milan 1964; J. Ackerman, *L'architettura di Michelangelo*, Turin 1968; *Michelangelo architetto*, edited by P. Portoghesi and B. Zevi, Turin 1964.

Among the popular works: B. Nardini, *Michelangelo. Biography of a Genius*, Florence 1999; M. Bussagli, *Michelangelo*, Florence 2000; *Exploring David. Diagnostic Tests and State of Conservation*, edited by S. Bracci, F. Falletti, M. Matteini and R. Scopigno, Florence 2004; C. Gamba, *Michelangelo*, Milan 2004; E. Capretti, *Michelangelo*, Florence 2006; C. Acidini Luchinat, *Michelangelo pittore*, Milan 2007; P. Dal Poggetto, *Michelangelo. La «stanza segreta». I disegni murali nella Sagrestia Nuova di San Lorenzo*, Florence 2012.

A fundamental support for the chronology of Michelangelo is K. Weil-Garris Brandt and N. Baldini in the catalogue of the exhibition *Giovinezza di Michelangelo* (annotated chronology), Florence 1999.

Catalogues of exhibitions:

Some exhibitions have provided an occasion for revisiting and closely examining the salient aspects of Michelangelo's biography, among them his apprenticeship and early activity: *Michelangelo e i maestri del Quattrocento*, edited by C. Sisi, Florence 1985; *Michelangelo e l'arte classica*, edited by G. Agosti and V. Farinella, Florence 1987; *Il giardino di San Marco. Maestri e compagni del giovane Michelangelo*, edited by P. Barrocchi, Cinisello Balsamo (Milan) 1992; *The genius of the Sculptor in Michelangelo's Work*, Montreal 1992; M. Hirst, J. Dunkerton, *Making and Meaning. The Young Michelangelo*, London 1994 (Italian edition, Modena 1994); *Giovinezza di Michelangelo*, edited by K. Weil-Garris Brandt with C. Acidini Luchinat, J. D. Draper, N. Penny, Florence-Milan 1999; *Michelangelo: grafia e biografia di un genio*, edited by L. Bardeschi Ciulich, Milan 2000; *Vita di Michelangelo*, edited by L. Bardeschi Ciulich, P. Ragionieri, Florence 2001; *L'ombra del genio. Michelangelo e l'arte classica a Firenze, 1537-1631*, edited by M. Chiarini, A. P. Darr, C. Giannini, Milan 2002; *Michelangelo: grafia e biografia. Disegni e autografi del maestro*, edited by L. Bardeschi Ciulich, P. Ragionieri, Florence 2002; *Venere e Amore. Michelangelo e la nuova bellezza ideale/Venus and Love. Michelangelo and the new ideawl of beauty*, edited by F. Falletti, J. K. Nelson, Florence 2002; *Michelangelo tra Firenze e Roma*, edited by P. Ragionieri, Florence 2003; *La Sistina e Michelangelo. Storia e fortuna di un capolavoro*, edited by A. De Strobel, G. Gentili, Milan 2003; *Vittoria Colonna e Michelangelo*, edited by P. Ragionieri, Florence 2005; *Il volto di Michelangelo*, edited by P. Ragionieri, Florence 2008; *Michelangelo architetto a Roma*, edited by M. Mussolin, Cinisello Balsamo (Milan) 2009.